HEARTBEAT

HOW I GREW FROM
VICTIM TO SURVIVOR

wishing you good health & peace..

MICHAEL DYMANT

iUniverse®

HEARTBEAT
HOW I GREW FROM VICTIM TO SURVIVOR

iUniverse books may be ordered through booksellers or by contacting:

iUniverse
1663 Liberty Drive
Bloomington, IN 47403
www.iuniverse.com
1-800-Authors (1-800-288-4677)

Because of the dynamic nature of the Internet, any web addresses or links contained in this book may have changed since publication and may no longer be valid. The views expressed in this work are solely those of the author and do not necessarily reflect the views of the publisher, and the publisher hereby disclaims any responsibility for them.

Any people depicted in stock imagery provided by Getty Images are models, and such images are being used for illustrative purposes only. Certain stock imagery © Getty Images.

ISBN: 978-1-5320-6867-6 (sc)
ISBN: 978-1-5320-6869-0 (hc)
ISBN: 978-1-5320-6868-3 (e)

Library of Congress Control Number: 2019902769

Print information available on the last page.

iUniverse rev. date: 03/07/2019

To my loving wife, Lynn, who always has my back.
And to Susan, teacher extraordinaire.

CONTENTS

AUTHOR'S NOTE

This story is based on my experiences in 2015 as I underwent two major cardiac surgeries to repair aortic aneurisms, a condition marked by an enlargement of the aorta. Ruptured aortas could be and are indeed often fatal.

I was thrown into the medical system and lost control of my life while I struggled with the physical and emotional challenges of my illness.

It is my hope that this collection of journal entries and other memories of my heart surgeries and recovery will help a variety of people. Nurses and caregivers, who are often the glue keeping patients from falling apart, will perhaps find their roles even more satisfying when they learn of the help I received from those like them and the difference they made.

Doctors, some of whom have earned my eternal gratitude, will understand what it's really like to be on the other side of the stethoscope and gain additional perspective as they care for their patients.

Those who are facing major surgery or already have survived it may find my story lessens their feelings of isolation and anxiety and brightens their outlook.

After all, if I came out whole and am having a life again, why wouldn't you?

(All the names of medical personnel have been changed for reasons of privacy.)

PROLOGUE

MAY 2018–VISITING DAY

The valet sends me a text with a code so that when I'm ready to leave, all I'll have to do is tap Reply to get my car back. I grab the box of Perugina chocolates I picked up as a gift and step out onto the pavement still impressed that I've driven here by myself. Granted, I used the car's GPS and the one on my iPhone as backup, but still.

I stroll through the broad entrance to the hospital, and my head instantly swivels to the left. *Hmmm. That's where I sat in the wheelchair waiting for Lynn to get the car. Who was the nurse who stayed with me?*

Remembering why I'm here, I refocus and walk over to the large desk staffed by two receptionists, one at each end. I look them over and pick the one who seems to be less grumpy.

"Good morning," I say with a smile when he looks up at me.

"Mornin'" is his less-than-cheerful reply.

"I was a patient here a few years ago, and I'm just visiting."

He puts down his pen and gives me a look. "So who are you visiting?"

"Well, no one in particular, just the cardiac ICU. That's where I stayed."

He picks up his pen and looks down at his desk. "Uh-huh," he mumbles, unimpressed. He takes my picture, hands me an ID, and directs me to the elevator bank.

"Which floor?" I ask half over my shoulder as I walk away.

"Two."

I've been meaning to do this, to come back here, for quite a while and for two reasons. One, to say thank you to the nurses who cared for me even though the ones who did may not be here today. I learned that it's a damned tough job being a nurse, especially on a ward like this, caught between doctors who often treat them like second-class citizens and clingy, frightened, bitchy patients. I sort of fell into the second camp. At least I think I did. Nurses rarely know what happens to patients who leave, so by showing up in one piece, I figure they can see the result of all their hard work. Actually, a ways back, my surgeon's nurse practitioner suggested it would be a good idea, and it appealed to me. So now I'm following through.

The other reason for making the visit is to face my remaining fears of this hospital. I suffered partial vision loss after my first surgery, so either Lynn, my wife, drives or I use a car service for longer trips, such as to

Manhattan or JFK Airport. But regardless of who does the driving, I'm getting sick of feeling that twinge of anxiety when the complex comes into view. I'm much better at dealing with this than I was a couple of years ago—I used to have near panic attacks then—but I want whatever leftover trauma there is purged from my psyche.

I did the same thing after my first wife, Susie, died. I went back to the hospital that had treated her uterine cancer and where she ultimately passed. I took the same route to get there, parked in the same lot as I had a hundred times before, walked to the oncology floor, and thanked the nurses. I recall that it helped me then. I hope repeating the exercise will help me now.

I step out of the elevator on the second floor, spot the arrow pointing the way to the CICU, and start walking. The hallway is busy with lots of people hustling to and fro, medical types in scrubs or white coats, civilians like me, some looking a bit dazed. I stop and notice a sign hanging from the ceiling. "Can I help you?" I look back down and see a young woman standing in front of me wearing a white coat, stethoscope, ponytail, and a broad smile.

Ever the charmer, I reply, "Yes."

"Oooh-kay, so where are you trying to go?" she asks.

I sheepishly explain my mission and punctuate it by showing off the box of chocolates I'm carrying.

"Let me walk you there," she says.

"Thanks."

I'm a man of few words when I'm not talking a blue streak.

A minute later, we come to an intersection and turn right into a short hallway. A pair of swinging doors labeled Cardiac Intensive Care Unit blocks the way. My guide steps ahead of me and pushes one of the doors open. "Right this way," she says. I take a deep breath and follow her in. *Here we go ...*

CHAPTER 1

MAY 2015—IS THIS REALLY ME?

I've been lying on my bed since lunch, two hours ago. Within arm's reach are the essentials every recovering cardiothoracic surgical patient ought to have—water, Extra Strength Tylenol, blood pressure monitor, cell phone, and TV remote. Plus in my case eyeglasses for distance and another pair for reading the Kindle or the *Wall Street Journal*, should I have the energy. I used to wear progressives, but my optometrist said I'd be better off à la carte. Something about the ministroke I had in surgery.

I carefully turn to the right toward the clock on my night table and see it's one forty-five. If she's on time, Susan should be here in fifteen minutes. Since it'll probably take me that long to get to the front door, I start to get up. Slowly, I push myself into a sitting position on the bed. I won't dare try using my abdominals or any other torso muscles; a deep surgical wound on my left side runs from my ribs to around my back and up to my clavicle. It's only two months old, and I'm deathly afraid it could open if I put any pressure on the area.

I sit on the edge of the bed for what feels like an hour waiting for the light-headedness to pass before I carefully make my way downstairs to the kitchen, one hand on the railing just in case. I fetch a bottle of water from the wine cooler and look out the window. A gray SUV pulls up in front of the house, and a woman carrying a briefcase and a shoulder bag emerges. This won't be my first adventure in psychotherapy, but it's shaping up to be the most important.

"Hi, Susan," I say with a little smile after opening the front door. She's somewhat older than me, perhaps in her late sixties, and she has a much bigger smile. "Would you like a bottle of water?" I ask, suddenly feeling guilty that I have one and she doesn't.

"I brought my own, see?" she replies, pulling an identical Poland Spring from her bag.

I nod and motion for her to follow me upstairs. My office, from which I've run an investment advisory practice for the past nineteen years, seems the right setting since it offers privacy. Plus a couch I can lie on.

"What a beautiful home," she says, surveying the living room.

"Thank you. Lynn gets the credit. She literally designed everything herself."

Susan knows of Lynn's gift for interior design. In fact, she knows a great deal about Lynn. She played an important role in helping Lynn cope with the loss of her mother in 2011. Now she's here to help me, though not with loss. I have a different type of trauma to deal with.

"Are you comfortable using my desk chair? Or you can sit on the couch and I'll use the chair. Or …"

Susan laughs. "The chair's fine for me."

I stop coming up with alternatives and carefully position myself on the couch first by sitting down, then swinging my legs over, and finally sliding my body backward until I reach the throw pillow. The whole production seems to take so long that I think our session may already be over. "Well," I grunt, "that wasn't easy."

Susan is sipping water and puts her bottle down. "You know, when you opened the door, I was amazed at how well you look."

"Really? I feel like I was in a plane crash."

Susan turns about as serious as anyone could. "You were."

A plane crash seems a fitting metaphor considering what I have gone through. A fifteen-hour surgery to repair a life-threatening aneurism and tear of the aorta in my abdomen and then to replace most of that network, leaving me with scars only Al Capone could love. The aneurism clocked in at a whopping seven centimeters, one and half times the size of a golf ball, and I learned the technical term: abdominal aortic aneurism, or triple A for short.

I spent four weeks in the hospital, half of them in solo ICU (cough and your nurse rushes in) and the rest in semiprivate, step-down ICU (press the Call button and start waiting). Considering I'd successfully avoided white coats most of my adult life to the point of being phobic, I'd had a lifetime of medical care compressed into a single month. And the worst part was that it wasn't over. In fact, that was only act 1.

While I lay semidelusional early on, Dr. Margolis, a member of my surgical team, asked me if I'd scheduled my second surgery yet. I was trying to process the first one and this guy was asking me about the next one? *What second surgery?*

Fortunately, Lynn intervened before the conversation went anywhere by asking Margolis to step out of the room with her. I wasn't worried. If she hurt him, there were plenty of other doctors around to patch him up.

I've been in therapy before, twice actually, so I know a thing or two about how to get the most out of it. First, admit there's a problem. Easy enough. I'm terrified of returning to the hospital to repair the two other aneurisms in my chest, but if I avoid the surgery for too long, I'll be dead. And since I firmly believe that being optimistic and upbeat increases the odds of success on the operating table, I need a 180-degree change in outlook. I also don't want the dread to follow me around like the Grim Reaper until I go back.

Finally, summer is my favorite time of year, and I want to enjoy it. So as I said, I have a serious issue to deal with, which brings me to the second admission: even though I know what needs to be done and why, I don't have the ability to effect the changes myself. Which explains why Susan is sitting across from me, pad and pen at the ready.

Since I love to talk, it seems natural for me to go first. "I just want to thank you for coming here. Pizza delivery is one thing, but therapy? I didn't think it possible."

Susan laughs at my little joke. I already see we'll be getting along fine. She's offered to treat me at home as a favor to Lynn, though with my screwed-up eyesight, keeping me off the road will probably save lives.

I suffered a partial vision loss called an optic neuropathy during my first surgery. Simply put, a rogue platelet crashed into an optic nerve and damaged it, not that anyone told me about rogue platelets until well after I reported my symptoms. I'd been complaining about things looking fuzzy while in ICU and heard "It's all that anesthesia" and "You haven't been in natural light for a while" as explanations from a pair of nurses. As I was cognitively dull as dirt, those theories made perfect sense to me, so I dropped the subject.

That is, until one evening in the semiprivate, step-down ICU when I was rubbing my left eye and noticed the digital clock on the wall had disappeared. "What the hell?" I said. When I took my hand away, the clock reappeared. "What the hell?" I repeated. Hand on eye, no clock. Hand not on eye, clock. No clock, clock—no clock, clock. *Okay, this isn't funny.*

I nearly tackled the next white coat I saw, a physician's assistant who strolled into my room to see my roommate the following morning. "Wait a minute," I said with enough drama to make her veer toward my bed. I described what was going on and illustrated it using my hide-the-clock moves. She listened closely. I hoped she was taking me seriously.

Apparently she was, because over the next few hours, I was visited separately by doctors from at least a half dozen departments with their respective residents in tow. At first, I sort of liked the attention. I didn't mind answering questions, performing my hide-and-seek act with the wall clock, or being subjected to a couple of field tests. My favorite was from one doctor who turned his hands into a pair of flying scissors that swooped down from each side while asking, "Can you see this?" After losing count of how many visits I'd had and with a CT scan thrown in for good measure, I was exhausted and annoyed. I had already called Lynn to report my symptoms. Now it was time to vent. I called her again.

"Anyone visit you so far about your eyes?" she asked right away.

"It would be easier to list who hasn't been in here," I moaned. "I've had it. They sent me for a scan too. Can you believe it? I didn't fall on my head."

Lynn rightfully ignored my complaints and got right to the point. "Just tell the next one who comes in that you're waiting to see the head of ophthalmology and then say goodbye."

It never occurred to me to boycott a medical exam. "Really?" I asked.

"Sure," she replied. "Just because you're available doesn't mean they have the right to keep questioning you."

Armed with my new Declaration of Independence, I eagerly awaited the next poor sap who had me on his list. It didn't take long.

"Mr. Dymant?" someone asked about five minutes after Lynn and I had hung up.

"Go check my file," I said without even looking up.

"Bye-bye."

Now that felt good.

Suddenly, a different type of memory bubbles up, and this time, I share it with Susan. "You know, I remember you from the bereavement group you ran. I went to only one meeting after my first wife died."

Susan nods. "I remember that."

"But what I especially recall was when I saw you alone first. Do you remember what you asked me?"

Susan shakes her head.

"You asked, 'And who's taking care of *you?*'"

I'm trying to hold back the tears, but they aren't cooperating. All I can do is choke out the words, "No one took care of me then. But now, Lynn does."

I spend the rest of the session relating to Susan exactly how I landed in the hospital.

"Lynn said you were in Miami when you had the attack."

"That's right. Imagine, I'm turning over on the massage table in the spa and it feels like someone ran me through with a sword. The pain was so severe I thought I'd faint. And it was only my first day there!"

Susan just looks at me, so I continue. "And for the next two weeks, I'm going to the gym, walking the beach, we're out to dinner every night …"

"And you didn't have pain?" she asks dumbstruck.

"Sure I did, but I just tried to ignore it. It was a freezing, snowy winter in New York and there I was in seventy-five-degree sunny Florida. No way I was going home early."

At this point, Susan must be wondering what sort of idiot she's dealing with.

"I get home a week before Lynn, and she texts me right away, 'How's your back?' I text back, 'Fine, no pain.'"

Susan stops sipping her water. "So you weren't being truthful?"

It's more of a statement than a question. I reach for my own water. "Actually, the pain really had subsided. I figured it was a kidney stone."

"But it wasn't."

"Not even close."

I move along with the story and explain how Lynn came with me for a CT scan and then to the urologist, who saw nothing wrong confirming my fantasy that I'd passed a kidney stone or better yet broken a world record for consecutive days of indigestion. Susan is finding this soap opera fascinating; she's leaning forward chin on fist like Rodin's *Thinker*.

"So," I say after taking a gulp of water, "we drive home, and I'm relieved—nothing more to worry about. That is, until the phone rings later that day. It's the urologist calling back. I figured that couldn't be just to chat."

"I don't imagine so," Susan says.

"He tells me that the radiologist found a large aneurism on the scan and that my cardiologist, Dr. Silver, was about to contact me. Right after I hang up, the phone rings again and sure enough it's the cardiologist.

'Michael,' he says firmly, 'drop what you're doing, pack a bag, and go to the hospital.' I'm walking from the bedroom back to the kitchen while he's talking. 'I'm just in the middle of cooking dinner,' I say like a dummy in denial. 'Drop what you're doing, pack a bag, and go,' Silver repeats."

Susan sits up straight when she hears this and asks, "You had some cardiac event earlier, right?"

"Yup," I say. "Technical term was an aortic dissection twelve years ago. Same thing happened to John Ritter, the actor, except he died and I survived. God knows why. Just so I could wind up under the knife and spend a month in hell? And now I have to go back to the same hospital."

I'm shaking my head and breathing faster, and my gut is doing flip-flops when I think of where I was two months previously and what happened to me. So much fear, the absolute terror I felt, the vulnerability, the pain, day after day after day … I snap out of my fog. "Sorry," I say, embarrassed. "Guess I zoned out a little."

Susan's smile warms up the room. "That's all right," she says, apparently having read my mind. "You're allowed to remember. In fact, I *want* you to remember everything you can and then keep expressing it."

I understand Susan's strategy. It helped me survive bereavement after my first wife died. Don't suppress the horrible memories; instead, get in touch with them. Doing so will purge the trauma and make for a happier, healthier me. Except for one thing.

"No problem," I say. "Day and night, I *can't* stop remembering, and I mean every damned detail, and I'll talk to just about anyone who'll listen, which is a pretty short list nowadays. I mean, I can't unload all the junk on Lynn every day."

Susan agrees. "That's true. But here in this safe space, you can at least unload it every week."

I pause and smile a little. Safe space. That sounds good to me, and it strikes me why. When you're rushed to the hospital for emergency surgery, you feel as if you've been kidnapped. One minute you're standing in your kitchen cooking dinner, and the next, you wake up in an ICU with a head full of drugs, twenty lines keeping you alive, and not a clue how you got there or what will happen next. Taken together, the last thing you feel is safe, and two months later, that sense of being at risk hasn't left me. In fact, I think it's intensifying.

Mixed in with flashbacks from my experiences in the hospital is a new preoccupation with death. I clearly managed to cheat it while I was in Florida as well as on the operating table in March. *But how many lives does a person get? What if something goes wrong today? Right now?* I wonder. *The tear in my aorta happened out of nowhere that day. What if it happens again?* The same fears followed me around twelve years previously. Guess that's where I got my training. I drove to a spa resort in the Berkshires by myself six months after my first "event" with my cardiologist's business card in my cup holder. That way, they'd know whom to call if I keeled over on the Taconic Parkway.

CHAPTER 2

SUMMER 2015–GETTING HELP (AND HOPEFULLY A TAN)

Susan has agreed to my request that we continue our two-hour sessions every Wednesday at two at my house. Implied is that the arrangement for therapy in the comfort of my own home would continue indefinitely making her the undisputed Mother Teresa of therapists.

Susan's office is only a twenty-minute drive away, and I know exactly where it is, but that's not the point. It's just that I'm still getting used to my new glasses and that my brain isn't sharp, so driving anywhere other than in my neighborhood is, well, let's just say I'm not ready. Maybe someday, but not yet.

Meanwhile, my limited driving is the least of my problems. Venturing out with Lynn to dinner, a movie, or a doctor's appointment—most places—creates enormous anxiety for me. The world seems the same as it always has, and yet it feels uneven, as if I might lose my balance and tip over. Or get lost and not know where to go. And that's when I'm *with* Lynn. The prospect of going anywhere outside my comfort zone by myself is enough to make me hyperventilate.

How long will I remain a prisoner of my fears? That's the primary question I keep posing as my weekly sessions with Susan continue. While we delve into the minefields of childhood that most therapists encourage patients to walk through, I continuously gravitate to my current laundry list of fears. Like my first post-op CT scan—*What if they find something, the alarms sound, and they throw me back into ICU?* The fifteen hours' worth of anesthesia I absorbed created hallucinations and paranoid ideations that lasted a good two weeks. Some felt so real that I couldn't be sure they weren't. Like the time I "saw" a scoreboard on the wall that displayed my vitals. Except the readings were impossible, like blood pressure at 2,500 over 1,000, which scared me to death at least in my hallucinations.

But what if I have my second surgery and become delusional again— and this time it won't go away? What if something happens to me in the middle of the night? What if something happens ... *and I'm alone?*

Susan seems to appreciate the significance to me of every matter I bring up no matter how absurd it may sound to anyone else, even Lynn. She's still taking care of me though I don't need nearly as much TLC as when I first came home from the hospital. But no one's patience is limitless.

I discover that the best way for me to deal with my fears is to stay in my comfort zone, meaning as much as possible staying home, where everything is familiar and I feel safe. Of course, it doesn't take long for that strategy to be tested when my office phone rings one afternoon. The voice on the other end delivers what should be exciting, wonderful news. Instead, it lands a one-two punch to my gut.

"The wedding is June 19th, and of course you're coming," says the voice.

I swallow hard and try to sound chipper. Only the father of the groom could buy it.

"I ... I mean we ... will absolutely be there."

This is a very important group of clients. They feel more like family actually, and they have for many years. So unless I'm back in the ICU, my tux will be heading for the dry cleaners. After a few *mazel tovs*, I get off the phone and find Lynn sitting in her office. She's researching an art class on her Mac while my panic is revving up.

"That was Manny. His son's wedding is June nineteenth, and he thinks I'll be showing up. Is he crazy? How in the world can I go?"

Lynn gives me one of those *Exactly how old are you?* looks. "We'll take a car service. It'll be fine. Where is it?"

"He mentioned a hotel in Midtown. I forget which."

"How many people?"

"At least a thousand."

"Oh."

I'm recounting the story of the wedding to Susan during our session the Wednesday after the affair. In fact, I launch into my narrative pretty much after saying hello.

"See, that's me in the tux," I crow, showing a cell phone pic of Lynn and me.

Susan squints at the screen and smiles. "You both look great."

"Thanks. Lynn posted it on her Facebook page with a heading about how far I've come. Fortunately, she left out the panic attack I almost had."

I explain that during the cocktail hour, Lynn went to the restroom while I resisted the urge to follow her. This resulted in my waiting alone near one of the bars for all of five minutes, which felt like five hours, hoping I wouldn't suddenly get dizzy and fall.

"So how did you deal with it?" Susan asks.

"I got a club soda and took a position leaning against a wall with the restrooms in view. And I kept telling myself, *She'll be back* over and over."

Susan smiles. "You handled that very well."

I look away. I mumble, "I was so embarrassed. Not that anyone knew what I was thinking. But still …"

Susan has been listening intently to my tale, but she isn't about to let me end it on such a sour note. "And what were the good things that happened?"

Now I'm smiling. "Well, I did get to see everyone I wanted to, and they all wished me well, said I looked good. And to see the groom walk down the aisle meant a lot to me since I remembered him as a boy."

Susan nods. "How long did you stay?"

"Let's see. The cocktail hour was more like two hours, and the ceremony was another hour. We skipped the reception and went home at that point. It would have been too much."

Susan puts her notepad in her lap and looks at me.

"So let's sum up. You made it to this very important affair, you socialized with people who are important to you, and you managed to keep it together when you weren't with Lynn. In other words, you did great!"

Now why couldn't I have said that?

This isn't the first time Susan has tried to get me to go easy on myself. And she hasn't been the only one to try to either. Lynn has been reminding me, and it feels I've been giving her a reason to every day. Whether it's misplacing my glasses, or tiring easily, or just forgetting the name of a movie we saw, my first reaction is invariably to beat myself up. I walk around calling myself an idiot under my breath and for what? Because I don't remember where I left something? Seems silly enough, and yet I can't seem to stop.

I've brought this up to Susan in session typically right after losing my train of thought. My frustration is more than obvious. "Dammit, what were we just talking about?" I blurt out one time after changing topics and then trying to recall how I got there. Susan gently reminds me of the original point I was making, but by then, I'm upset. "You'd think by now I wouldn't still be dealing with this," I say angrily. "It's been three months already since the surgery."

Susan shakes her head. "Michael, after what you've been through, three months is nothing. Fifteen hours of anesthesia, gallons of other medications, the hypothermia that helped you survive while the surgery took place—you have to give it at least a year before you can even think about your cognitive abilities."

Surprising information. "Really?"

"Oh yes. And your cognitive abilities are actually quite good. Your speech and vocabulary are excellent, and your job requires complicated math skills. Sure, you're a little fuzzy, and there are some short-term memory issues, but anyone who went through what you have would be lucky to have just the problems you're having."

Well, when you put it that way, who am I to complain?

The summer moves along, and I'm enjoying it relatively speaking. Not knowing exactly when my second surgery will take place is giving me peace of mind—as long as I don't think about it. Unfortunately, I think about it. A lot. Still, I've developed a manageable routine comprising morning walks down the block and back listening to my iPod, working until lunch, and then napping on my deck in the afternoon or inside on the couch if it's raining.

Seth, my assistant, is still working for me thank God. That relieves me of some of the pressure and replaces it with laughs as well as spirited political exchanges. He leans left while I lean right, but we haven't killed each other as of this writing. And Lynn and I have been venturing out to dinner together more often; I've even had a glass of wine a few times. Well, I sip it for an hour, and it hits me like a sledgehammer, but that still counts. And of course I'm having my sessions with Susan every Wednesday.

We're planning a late-summer vacation to Ocean House, a beautifully restored resort hotel on the beach in Rhode Island we've been to before. It's just the sort of getaway I need, and though I'd prefer guaranteed weather in a place like Anguilla, getting on a plane that soon after surgery wouldn't be a smart idea. Lynn will have to do the driving, but it's only a couple of hours from our house. For this trip to happen, however, I'll have to clear some major hurdles.

First up is my initial post-op CT scan to be performed in a building adjacent to the hospital complex. Lynn is sitting with me in the crowded waiting area reading her iPad while I'm wondering what my heart rate is.

My name is called, and as I start to get up, she gives me a quick kiss. "Good luck," she says with a smile.

"Thanks," I reply nervously and head for the check-in station.

A tech is waiting for me, and we go through a pair of doors. I change into a gown, get jabbed with an IV, and take a seat in another waiting area. A male patient sits across from me. He's about my age. We exchange nods no doubt each wondering why the other is here. I'm practicing deep breathing in an effort to remain calm, but it's not working very well since I'd like to run outside and find the car. But I don't have the keys. So I wait for my name to be called again. That takes about ten hours. Well maybe it was just ten minutes.

The tech who comes for me has a nice smile, which I take as an invitation to start my nervous chatter as I follow her into the exam room. "You know, this is my first scan since I was discharged. I mean, I had quite a few while an in-patient. In fact, my first one was—"

"Okay, Mr. Dymant. Let's get you up on the table."

I guess chatter time is over.

It's a nerve-racking hour. I keep expecting sirens to go off meaning that some life-threatening discovery has been made. But once I'm sitting with Lynn over coffee and a croissant at the hospital's food court, I realize I'm in the clear. The relief I feel is overwhelming, and I can sense a nap coming on. Of course getting only three hours of sleep last night could be the reason.

Next up is an appointment with Dr. Vesci, a vascular surgeon referred to me by the cardiothoracic surgeon's office. There's been some swelling in my left foot and calf, so I might need an area of my upper leg drained, a procedure I endured without too much fuss while I was an in-patient back in March.

I've already had an ultrasound test, and we've brought the results. Lynn and I exchange pleasantries with the good doctor while handing over the printout. After a quick physical exam of the area in question, we're back in our seats across from him.

Vesci leans forward and steeples his fingers. "Draining usually isn't a solution. So before we just cut you open ..." is how he begins. Really.

I get a sudden case of lockjaw while I'm wondering if Lynn is getting ready to swing her shoulder bag at his head. This is likely to get ugly in a hurry, and Vesci is about to make matters a whole lot worse. Lynn asks why since I'll be on the table for surgery 2 anyway he can't just perform this drainectomy at the same time. I like the idea of making my next visit to the hospital a two-for-one special but can't seem to verbalize it since my mouth still isn't working. Vesci offers a patronizing smile. "I don't think I'd do that," he says. "Just because he came out whole after the first surgery doesn't mean he will the second time around."

I'm amazed Lynn hasn't leaped across the desk and grabbed him by the lapels.

"Now you listen to me," she says through gritted teeth, and I've been on the receiving end of that voice a few times. Trust me. It's not pretty. "Where do you come off speaking to my husband like that? Do you have even the faintest idea of what he's been through? *Well do you?*"

The doctor is in shock. I feel like I was being mugged and Batgirl has just shown up. I lean back in my chair and cross my arms across my chest to show Vesci how tough I can be too. The combined effect seems to be more than he can take. He changes his tune faster than a speeding bullet.

"You know," he says making more eye contact with Lynn than me since he sees her as the bigger threat, and I think he's probably right about that. "Michael looks terrific all things considered."

I give him a little wave. "I'm right over here."

"Oh yes of course," he says, clearing his throat. "What I meant to say is that very often, these cysts drain on their own just from the patient being ambulatory. Yours was drained the first time in the hospital because you were in bed so much of the time."

I like where this is going. I uncross my arms. "So what are you saying exactly?"

"Let's wait a month and then have another ultrasound. The cyst might be smaller, in which case we'll be happy we left it alone."

I think, *You mean left me alone, don't you?*

It takes quite an effort to say thank you as Lynn and I leave the office, but it's a real simple matter for me to rip Vesci's business card in half as we head for the elevator.

"I won't let that guy near me," I say.

"I won't either," says Lynn.

So it's all systems go for our beach vacation, which we've booked for the last week in August. My internist, who I've shown my swollen leg to, has told me that she sees lots of patients my age and older with the same issue in the summer and especially those who've been taking one of the blood pressure meds I'm taking. So with my cardiologist's okay, I've dropped that pill. And within a matter of days, my leg returns more or less to normal. Now I have to figure out a way to get even with the vascular surgeon who seemed to go out of his way to scare the crap out of me. *What was his specialty in medical school? Sadism?*

I've gotten past this episode and my resulting anger and chosen instead to focus on the trip and everything about it I expect to enjoy, especially sun worshipping, weather permitting. Lynn and I have joined a local health club with an outdoor pool for the summer. At first, I'm uncomfortable taking off my T-shirt. Due to the giant wrap-around scar front to back and assorted small ones on my chest, I was self-conscious to say the least. But as the weeks roll by and my desire to get a tan increases, I'm developing a *Who cares?* attitude and have begun to think of my scars as badges of courage, my personal collection of Purple Hearts. Still, I've already prepared a few explanations in case anyone notices how I look while I'm on the beach. *Oh this? I saved a child from a lion attack while on safari.* Or *I was an extra in a Freddy Kruger movie and there was a slipup.* And my favorite, *You think you're tough? Survive this, and then you can talk to me!*

But my self-confidence is fleeting, and I suppose I shouldn't be surprised. This will be a trip way out of my comfort zone. Though my physical recovery has been on target, I'm still a fragile, overripe peach emotionally. In fact, I'm still having powerful flashbacks and nightmares about my hospital stay—not as often, but they keep showing up usually at night, when I'm at my most vulnerable. For the first few weeks after I got home, I would often bolt awake in the darkness with a yell, waking Lynn.

"I'm sorry," I mumbled one time, trying to figure out what had happened.

"Bad dream?" she asked though it wasn't really a question.

"Yeah. I was driving and got stuck on a drawbridge that was opening. So if I went forward or backward, I'd crash. And the bridge kept opening wider. Now where the hell did that come from? I'm barely even driving yet!"

I've been raising the fear subject with Susan more often lately since the trip date is coming closer. "This will be my first vacation since the surgery. You'd think all I'd be is excited," I say after we get past our hellos and what's new intro one Wednesday in early August. Susan smiles as if she's been expecting to hear me say this, but she doesn't offer any wisdom just yet, so I continue.

"I mean, really. It's not like we're going to Bora Bora. It's just a couple hours away by car. And we've been there before." My frustration is in full gear now. "Why the hell is everything so hard? Is it me?"

This sort of down talk is of course Susan's natural trigger point and she's having none of it. "No, it's not you," she says firmly, "not in the sense you mean—that there's something wrong with you."

I'm not in a very accepting mood. "No? Then what the hell is it?"

Susan gives me one of those serious looks. "You're being way too hard on yourself. You're evaluating yourself as if nothing has happened." She leans forward, and I do likewise. "In other words, you're not being fair to yourself."

"Which means I should do what?"

"Give yourself a break."

I know Susan's right. We've covered this territory numerous times. That we're still covering it is a perfect example of just how thick my skull must be, though to be fair, it's not that I don't understand the concept. It's just that I instantly knee-jerk before I can gauge what the risks to me of a situation are.

"How much of this is connected to my experiences in the hospital?" I ask her.

Susan nods. "I'm sure there's a connection. To what degree I don't know exactly. But there's a connection."

Of course, the real question is what I can do about it. Susan's answer surprises me in that it's simple and utterly obvious. "You're a writer."

"So?"

"So write."

A writer? I wouldn't exactly label myself as such though I did tell Susan I'd penned a memoir and had it published ten years previously. Well, self-published. Anyway, I entered it in a couple of national contests, and it was recognized. So sure, I'm a writer. Why not?

I look at Susan. "You know, I miss writing. I really enjoy it. You think I should put my nightmares on paper?"

"I do. It's another way to purge the memories and heal."

"Okay, but it's a little scary. Every horrible detail and all my feelings will come out."

"That's the idea."

CHAPTER 3

LATE SUMMER 2015– THE PURGE BEGINS

Susan leaves at four in the afternoon, her usual time, and after seeing her to the front door, I consider going back to my office to start typing. But I really should feed the dogs. I'm tempted to do neither and have a nap instead, yet I somehow find myself in front of the keyboard staring at a blank page on Word. I give it a title, close my eyes, and let the memories begin to seep out.

Medical Journals

How helpless do I feel lying here in this hospital bed? And what type of sadist designed it anyway? I'm so uncomfortable. No, miserable. I have a catheter coming out of my privates, a surgical wound held together with dozens of staples that I can't even see most of since it goes from my side all the way around up my back and then to my clavicle. So if I try to sit up, I need the damned control pad. If I want to roll onto my side, either side, well, that would make sense since I must be a masochist.

So I try to lie still as that's the way to avoid the pain, but I can't do that indefinitely, since I need ... **Shit. What do I need? Can't remember**. I'm so fuzzy. My head doesn't work. Something Lynn told me to ask the nurse practitioner when I see her, but what? Oh, maybe I wrote it down. Yes, that's it. I did! Now where the hell is that clipboard? Naturally, its somewhere on that stupid rolling table along with four cups of water, a box of tissues, yesterday's **Wall Street Journal**, my iPod, eyeglasses, and God knows what else.

Sticking out from this landfill—hooray!—I see the clipboard. It's just out of reach, and I can't get the table to roll over to the bed. It's like one of those supermarket shopping carts with wobbly wheels, so I'll have to use the control pad to call for help ...

Thanks. Now I feel a hundred percent useless as my conversation with some nail-file-wielding, coffee-drinking, yawning, fired-from-last-job (You want fries with that?) person who answers *my Call button via a speaker on the wall across the room begins. If only I could sleep until it's time to go home. And they call this step-down ICU—more like I stepped in something else. So the question remains, how helpless do I feel? And while I'm at it, how the hell did I wind up here?*

The next day, I open up the file I've created, Medical Journals, on Word and reread what I've written. I lean back in my chair and type some more.

I'm looking at the wall clock that sits halfway between my bed and my roommate's, the logic being each of us deserves an equal shot at seeing it from an angle. Watching the yellow LED readout has become one of my favorite activities as well as one of my most hated. On one hand, I use it to count the hours until Lynn will come see me. She always ballparks it for me because she knows how her visits are one of the few things that are keeping me sane. She also never arrives empty-handed—she brings real food, real coffee (not the brown shit they serve here), and the latest Wall Street Journal.

But what I love most are the cards and especially the ones from her with inspirational messages such as "You got this!" Each time I read one, I cry. The wall and shelves across from my bed are covered with them, and naturally, I can never reach the tissues, which are somewhere on the table. So as the time counts down to Lynn's daily arrival, usually late afternoon—though early on she was there twice a day—my mood elevates in lockstep.

But that clock has an evil side to it—nighttime. By nine or so, Lynn has left for home and some much-needed rest. If my roommate has had any visitors, they've gone too, and as a courtesy to him, I'm not turning on my TV. That and because the remote is such a piece of junk I could break a finger trying to change channels. So I'm left with my Kindle and Notebook both fully charged thanks to Lynn. But lurking in the back of my mind is the fear—no, the certainty—that I won't be able to fall asleep.

And so my nightly ritual begins ... Read a few book chapters, look at the clock, curse, watch a Netflix movie, look at the clock, curse, endure late-night meds and needles, look at the clock, curse ... I don't think it's physically possible to stay awake for a week or more straight. Or maybe it is because that's what it feels I've been doing.

Friday afternoon, I sit down and type until my fingers hurt.

They call it ICU psychosis or hospital psychosis. I guess the latter means it extends from the ICU through the step-down ICU until you're in the parking lot in street clothes going home. Really. After I'm paroled after four weeks in this joint, my ability to discern reality is about the same as a hamster that's been deprived of natural light. Both of us are incredibly confused, and neither of us can have a normal BM. The digestion issue will be easily resolved, I suppose. I'll just need to eat some good food, get a decent night's sleep, and take something over the counter.

The confusion is another matter altogether, and I hardly know how to tackle it. So I strain to pull up memories. I figure that if I can put them in some sort of chronological order, a natural tactic for a type-A guy like me, the fog will lift. Problem is when I do, I desperately try to get them back out of my head because they're too damn terrifying to keep in plain view. Maybe I could do a better job if I weren't so incredibly tired. I've never been so tired. In fact, the word **tired** doesn't do it justice. The slightest exertion—just getting out of bed to go to the bathroom and having breakfast—propels me into a multihour nap.

27

Meanwhile, back to the psychosis. If you never believed in the boogeyman or were never afraid to look under the bed, all you need to do is experience what I did. You'll believe all right.

I haven't corrected this many spelling errors since kindergarten. But I don't care. I just want to keep writing.

If only someone had warned me that fifteen hours of anesthesia plus enough chemicals pumped into me around the clock to make the CEO of Monsanto proud would likely change my brain chemistry. Was that too much to ask? Between the time I was admitted on a Monday night and the time they wheeled me into the OR four days later, I'm sure there were a few opportunities for a heads-up. I mean, it's not like I was busy. If someone had said, "Mr. Dymant, I just want you to be aware of the possible side effects of being put under," I wouldn't have responded, "Gee, I'm really sorry, but can't we talk some other time? I was just getting the hang of the TV remote." If any of the surgeons, anesthesiologists, physicians' assistants, nurse practitioners, aides, or even a janitor had just given a damn, maybe I could have dealt with the hallucinations, delusions, and paranoia just a teensy bit better. If any one of them had made an effort to ground me when I saw Lynn's spirit float across the ceiling or felt trapped under a descending air vent that would surely crush me to death. Didn't anyone notice me conversing with imaginary foods that moved? Overhear my crying panic that came with my "realization" of losing my wife, business, money, and freedom? Hadn't anyone found it odd when I spit out pills and accused my nurse of setting me up as a drug user and dealer? How about when I tried to leave the hospital since my arrest was inevitable and I just wanted to get it over with? Was everyone just so damned busy with their charts and laptops and statistics to remember that somewhere under the rumpled sheets surrounded by tubes and wires and monitors was a man scared half out of his mind?

I take the weekend off from journaling. In fact, I decide to wait until after my next session with Susan. That Wednesday morning, I print everything I've written so far, staple it all together, and leave it on my desk. Like a grade-school student who's finished his assignment, I'm anxious to show off my work.

Susan arrives on time, and we go into my office.

"What shall we do with these?" I ask waving the papers in the air with a grin.

"My, you've been busy," Susan replies with a smile. "We can do with them whatever you like. Including nothing at all."

I shake my head. "I'd rather we read them. Better yet, you read them out loud and I'll just lie here on the couch."

It takes Susan a good half hour to finish, and that's not because she's a slow reader. Rather, we keep stopping so I can get through my crying jags that seem to erupt with each paragraph. After she reads the last page, I manage to compose myself and look at her. One of her hands is clutching the journals and the other rests on her chest as if she were reciting the Pledge of Allegiance. Neither of us seems able to speak, but I know we're both thinking the same thing: *Wow!*

Now I'm even more motivated to keep writing, and it seems I'm doing so every day. What was once a trickle is turning into a stream.

> There are twenty-four hours in a day, and since I'm awake for most of them, time crawls with the speed of a drunken snail. In a desperate attempt to move the calendar along, I've learned to chop up the day into a series of events I can look forward to. First on the list naturally is the next visit from Lynn, and when that's but a few hours off, I begin counting down by fixating on the wall clock.
>
> My older daughter has been bringing lunch for both of us during her lunch hours a few times a week, so I use the same clock countdown method for her visits too. Incredibly, those are the only activities that are predictable time-wise, though in all fairness, I should include the three delivered meals each of which creates a side activity—betting on whether or not they deliver exactly what I ordered. I consider involving my current roommate—"I'll give

you five to one they forget to toast my English muffin"—but I don't. The poor guy has had a quadruple bypass, and though everyone says my surgery was the most taxing to the human body possible, I don't think he's in the mood for the step-down casino.

I'm sure that being a nurse's aide is a lousy occupation—dealing with cranky patients, emptying bedpans, and handling other assorted undignified tasks and for low pay and no glory, but hey—no one forced them to take the job. Okay, I don't want to strangle all of them. Just some. Especially Clarice, who makes me cringe whenever I see her name on the board across from my bed. As friendly as an IRS agent, she can't muster an audible hello and must have forgotten how to smile years ago. I ignore her as best I can whenever she's assigned to my room, but one evening, I nearly lose it.

Roger, my quad-bypass roommate, makes the mistake of posing a simple request—a blanket. Clarice grunts an assent, fetches one from the closet, and casually tosses it on the foot of Roger's bed. "Would you please cover me?" he asks because he's as much a tangle of wires and tubes as I am. "Cover yourself" is her reply, and she quickly leaves the room.

Overhearing this, I think a sequel to my delusions has been released. "Roger, I can't believe that bitch," I say through the curtain that divides us. "If I could get out of this damn bed, I'd cover you myself."

They should make aides wear hats with built-in audiovisual recorders like cops have to. If they did, maybe Clarice would be working at the DMV instead of this hospital. I think she'd fit in there perfectly.

Susan and I read through these latest journals, and she doesn't need to point out to me just what theme is running through them—anger. And since I'm such a consistent, predictable guy, I don't stray much from that theme when I return to the keyboard that weekend.

Lynn is standing by the foot of my bed and looks down. "When's the last time someone changed your socks?" she asks referring to the hospital footwear with the nonskid soles that are always on upside down. Since my brain has the consistency of an overripe cantaloupe, I just shrug. She yanks them off and recoils at the sight of my feet, which based on her reaction I figure have been somewhat neglected these past few weeks.

"And what about the gown?" she continues. "I could figure out today's menu just by looking at it."

"Gimme a break!" I shoot back. "My coordination stinks worse than my feet! But I know what Lynn is getting at—it's all the care and attention they're **not** paying me, not a critique of my personal hygiene. She storms out of the room, and I'm almost feeling sorry for whoever will be in her crosshairs. Almost but not quite.

Half an hour later, Lynn's back. She announces that she's filed a formal complaint with the hospital. My brain is yelling, **You go, girl!** but what comes out of my mouth is "Great. I hope they don't take it out on me. This place is bad enough already." Turns out complaints like these can't be ignored since reports and funding are joined at the hip. Who knew?

The next morning after another botched breakfast delivery, a pleasant-looking aide in her twenties walks into the room, stops at the foot of my bed, looks at me, and smiles. I figure she must be auditioning for a part in a movie, but no, she's for real. "Good morning, Mr. Dymant," she chirps brightly. "I'm Sheryl. I thought you might like some personal care."

If this is another delusion, it's the nicest one so far. "Okay, what do you have in mind?" I ask.

Sheryl crooks a finger under her chin pretending to think. This girl's got my sense of humor. "Hmm, let's see. You could use a shave, so let's start there. Then I'll dry wash your hair and give you a sponge bath. Oh, and I have some nice lotion for a foot massage. How's that sound?"

I take it all in and smile back at Sheryl. "You go, girl!" I say.

An hour later, she's gathering the used towels when I offer to pay her if she'll repeat this spa performance daily. I know she won't accept the bribe, but what I learn is that I'm entitled to this type of care; it's just a matter of demanding it.

Just for a change, I read this installment aloud while lying on the couch and Susan sits in my desk chair and listens. I don't cry at all. In fact, I actually find myself laughing for once. Susan has been chuckling too.

"Did you really offer to pay the aide? That's hilarious," she says.

"I did. When I look back on it, I guess it was pretty funny."

Susan and I exchange a look.

"Maybe there was more to this experience than trauma. Could that be?" she asks.

It feels like it takes me forever to answer. "I don't know. Maybe."

The next time I sit down to write, I make a conscious effort to recall something positive about my hospital stay. Of course, the fact I'm alive ought to be the first thought that comes to mind; I was lucky to survive the surgery in the first place. But my brain is still having trouble shifting into gratitude mode, so that's not where I go. Instead, I pull up another memory, but interestingly, it's not such an awful one.

It's time I walk farther than the fifteen feet to the bathroom. Yes, despite knowing I'll have to drag the IV pole with one hand in public and that a bag of pee clipped to it that's connected via a

tube to my catheter will be on display, I'm determined to at least
see the outside world if I can't be in it. And that means I'll have
to make it to the end of the hall and get past a half dozen other
rooms and the nurses' station to reach the patients' lounge where
I'm told—drum roll please—there are windows! I haven't looked
through one since I arrived at the ER, which must be at least
two weeks ago. Or is it less? Or more? I've no idea since I can't
keep a semblance of a calendar in my head. Anyway, it's not
that my room doesn't have a window; it does. It's just that my bed
isn't up against it, and with the curtain drawn between the beds,
I simply can't see it. So I've become increasingly determined to
see outside, which explains my damn-the-torpedoes-full-speed-
ahead mentality. I'm going to walk to the lounge if it kills me.

Of course, all the bravado in the world won't unhook the wires and
tubes I can temporarily survive without, which means I'll need help,
which means I'll have to talk to the speaker grill on the wall, which
means I'd rather yank everything out of my body myself and take
my chances. But I don't because suddenly there's a smiling face
across from me at the foot of the bed. Could I be in for another spa
treatment? Her ID tag is a blur thanks to my screwed-up vision, but
the mystery is quickly cleared up when she says her name is Judy
and announces, "I'm from physical therapy."

I start to sit up, which is no easy chore. "Okay, Judy," I say,
"let's hit the road."

After an aide rearranges my wires and gizmos, Judy helps me to
my feet. I'm wobbly, and it takes me a minute before I feel stable
enough to get going. "Hang on a sec," Judy says. "We, um, need
to keep you properly covered if you know what I mean."

I don't know what she means, at least not right away, but then
I realize my gown is open at the back.

"I'll be right back," she says as she rushes out of the room presumably to find something appropriate for me to wear so as not to offend anyone.

Actually, I think taking a stroll with my ass sticking out is probably just the comic relief this depressing ward needs, and I tell Judy just that when she returns with another gown. "Somehow, I don't think so," she laughs, and I join in. They say laughter is good for the soul, so I've been trying to keep my sense of humor. It's not easy, but being a wiseass is helping me stay sane these days.

Judy maneuvers my arms into the sleeves of the gown backward, like a normal shirt, and after she ties it up, the risk of my giving any nurses or wandering patients a peek is eliminated.

Off we go. Well, that's being generous since it sounds like we're really motoring. Actually, if I were going any slower, it would be backward. Judy has my right arm firmly in her grasp, which makes me feel pretty darn good since I might keel over without her. I can't believe how exhausting this is, and we're only halfway down the hall. I feel like I'm wearing lead shoes. My leg muscles have the tone of wet noodles.

"How are you feeling so far?" Judy asks.

"Fine," I lie. I'm afraid she'll abort Mission Windows if I let on, and who knows when I'll get my next chance. Then again, I won't be able to appreciate the view if I pass out and hit the floor, so I call for a time-out. "Can I take a minute?" I ask breathing heavily. "Then we can keep going."

"Sure thing," Judy replies. She's so nice that I'm amazed she actually works here.

"Well, that journal entry was inspirational."

Those are Susan's first words after reading it aloud the following week. "Really?" I ask. "Why do you say that?"

Susan puts her pad and pen in her lap and leans forward. "You were so determined to get to the windows that nothing was going to stop you. I can only imagine how frightening it must have been to take that walk even with the physical therapist."

I shrug in agreement. "I guess it was." I get off the couch, walk to my desk, and pick up another sheet of paper I had cleverly left there upside down. "Surprise!" I say. "One more."

Overall, I'm probably being a little too harsh in my recollection of the various behaviors of the hospital staff. While most of the doctors are aloof and some of the aides would be better suited to flipping burgers than taking care of patients, there have been some truly caring and compassionate nurses. And not just in the ICU, where it's practically a given. Or at least ought to be. But the step-down unit is understaffed, so those there are more easily overwhelmed. And the step-down is where I need the most emotional care.

In ICU, I spent a good deal of time lost in a sea of delusions and hallucinations visual and auditory, and as terrifying as that was, I don't know if any nurse could have managed to ground me. Who knows? Maybe some of them did try and I just don't remember.

I do remember being aware that my wrists were tied to the bed railings and concluding that it was to prevent me from falling. Gallons of chemicals flowing to the brain can do that to a person. Of course, Lynn told me the real story. "You were trying to leave the hospital and go home," she said. "It took four nurses to hold you down. I think two were male." I was in disbelief yet picturing the action made me laugh. I mean really—a sixty-one-year-old Jewish investment adviser tough guy wrestling the whole ICU staff?

So it's hard to fully recall the nursing staff in ICU since I can't distinguish my delusional from my real memories of them. I do recall one nurse asking me if I was ready to try some liquids, and being as parched as the Gobi Desert, I yelled "Yes!" Except it came out completely garbled since I was hoarse from the breathing tube that had finally been removed. I'm sure she was able to read my answer by looking at me, and a few minutes later, a smorgasbord was presented for my approval—water, apple juice, Jell-O, and lemon ices. I greedily inhaled each and begged for seconds. "Another lemon ice?" she asked.

"Oh God, this tastes like Möet & Chandon champagne," I croaked. "Yes please!" She removed the debris from my table and with a smile went to fetch my refill. If I hadn't looked like hell and no doubt smelled even worse and had had any strength at all, I would have hugged her when she returned. Though in truth, I just wanted that lemon ice.

CHAPTER 4

FALL 2015—READY, SET ...

Before I know it, October 27 will be here and I'll be back where I started—in ICU having been sliced and diced yet one more time. Okay, back where I started isn't quite accurate since my first round of surgery was an emergency and this time I've chosen the when, where and who so it won't *become* an emergency.

But rationalizations aside, it sure feels I'll have gone full circle even if I can list the differences between then and what's reasonable for me to expect in round 2. Last time, I stayed a whopping four weeks, half in the ICU and the rest in the step-down ICU.

The forecast this time is more like ten to fourteen days. The first surgery had me under for a dozen hours plus three more the next day to finish closing me up. This time, I'll be flat on my back for perhaps five hours. Last time, I was on my side and at a forty-five-degree angle head generally pointing down. Good thing I never saw what I looked like since a few months later, Lynn told me I had swelled to the point of being unrecognizable and had turned blue from being subjected to hypothermia. Sort of like a Smurf balloon in the Thanksgiving Day Parade.

The shorter surgery will mean less time I'll be put under, so I shouldn't suffer from paranoia, delusions, and hallucinations again. So all in all, I should get through this surgery easier, get home sooner, and recover faster. That's what I keep telling myself.

What I've also concluded is more of a spiritual matter. I've decided that if God wanted to be done with me, he or she would have knocked me off back in March. After all, what type of sadist would put me through all that misery and let me slowly recover just to bring me back seven months later to finish the job? I mean, really. God has better things to do.

This is the speech I make with Susan, my captive audience during one session in September in an attempt to give my "It won't be such a big deal" storyline some legs. Actually, I've been telling anyone who'll listen to the condensed version of the same thing though I don't think the purpose has been to persuade anyone. It's really been to convince myself. All part of my belief that a positive outlook will raise the odds of my survival. I have no idea where I got that; I certainly don't recall reading it anywhere. Still, it sounds right to me.

Something else I don't know is what made the calendar turn so fast. One minute I'm on the beach in Rhode Island enjoying terrific weather, getting a tan, and just feeling pretty darn good about myself. That's because my second surgery feels like it's decades off. And then, just like that, I can feel it coming closer. I'm trying to keep my game face on each day, but bravado has never been my strong suit.

The Jewish High Holidays arrive midmonth, and we go back to Temple Shaaray Tefila, a Reform synagogue. For someone like me brought up Conservative bordering on Orthodox, attending a Reform *shul* is about as likely as a rabbi ordering a ham sandwich. Yet here I sit one more time with Lynn during the Rosh Hashanah service. She convinced me to give Reform a try last year, and I nearly swore I wouldn't go back. That the rabbi was female didn't bother me, but her sermon linking Judaism to yoga did. I mean, yoga? Seriously? And a cantor playing a folk guitar? *Where am I? La-La Land?*

But oddly enough, my cynicism seems to be melting away as soon as the service begins. I have no idea why. The rabbi is the same, but now, I feel a certain warmth emanating from her. The cantor is strumming that guitar again as he sings, yet this time, I find myself appreciating the quality of his voice. And with each prayer that's recited, whether in Hebrew or English, I feel my own heartstrings being plucked. The same prayers I've recited for more than fifty years that never affected me— well, suddenly they are. *What the heck is going on?* I ask myself. I turn slightly to my right. I'm curious if Lynn is reacting in any way, but if she is, I can't tell. I reach into my suit pocket to find my handkerchief. I want to be ready for the flood because I'm sensing it's not far off. The next prayer tells me I'm right.

It's actually a poem that asks, "Who shall live and who shall die?" the next year. And if that load isn't heavy enough, it not only lists a variety of causes such as fire, drowning, or stoning; it also poses other questions, such as who will be poor, or in bad health, or alone. It's too much for me to bear, and I'm choking as each question is posed. My left hand, the one that located the handkerchief, is now fully occupied trying to keep up with the tears streaming down my face. And I find my right hand is suddenly intertwined with Lynn's. We look at each other and smile. Our hands remain clasped until the service ends.

We're quiet in the car on the way home. That is, until Lynn makes a single comment. "You were quite vulnerable back there."

I gaze straight ahead and nod. Fortunately, I have more than one handkerchief.

The caller ID reads Medical, so it must be my surgeon's office calling to remind me not to eat or drink anything tonight since tomorrow is my big day. I'm half-right.

"Hello, Joyce," I say as soon as I recognize her voice right after she says hello. "Calling to review my dos and don'ts?"

"Not exactly," she replies. "I'm sorry to tell you this, but your surgery is postponed by one day."

I'm stunned. "Why?"

"Well, Dr. Somerset has an unavoidable procedure for tomorrow. He told me to tell you he promises the delay will be only one day."

I thank Joyce and hang up. I'm not exactly sure how I feel about this development. On the one hand, I was really pumped up to go in tomorrow morning. I've been working on it in therapy for weeks, and by now, I can recite my "This surgery will be no big deal" speech in my sleep. Now, I'll have the extra time to kill, which will give me plenty of opportunities to think and get nervous. On the other hand, I won't have to fast until tomorrow night, which means ...

"Lynn?"

"Yeah?"

"Let's make a reservation at Benjamin's Steakhouse."

"For when?"

"Tonight."

"Huh?"

Now that my carnivorous side has been addressed, I quickly fire off a text to Susan. "Guess what? My surgery is postponed a day!"

She quickly replies, "Would you like a pep talk?" to which I answer, "Please!"

A half hour later, I'm pacing around on the driveway with my cell phone plastered to my ear.

"You made it through the first time, and that's because you're strong," Susan says. "You'll get through this too."

I believe her and tell her so. Before signing off, I promise to journal everything that happens in round 2. She believes me and tells me so.

CHAPTER 5

... GO!

The alarm sounds at 4:30 a.m. I slap it off before it wakes Lynn. Somehow, I've managed to sleep four or five hours—and without a Xanax too, though my beta-blocker, which slows my heart rate, may have helped.

I stumble into the bathroom and find the surgical wipes the nurse practitioner gave me. I'm supposed to use them to prevent infection, but I wonder if I'm qualified. Squinting at the microscopic wording, I follow the instructions and scrub my arms, legs, and chest. Brushing my teeth is followed by splashing water on my face in a useless attempt to wake up. I get dressed, grab my overnight bag, and head downstairs to take care of the dogs.

An hour later, I'm ready to roll, as is Lynn, who's sipping a coffee in the kitchen. I consider sneaking half a cup: *What could be the harm?* But I know better than to try it. Instead, I remember there's a restaurant in the hospital, so I vow to wipe out their coffee inventory as quickly as possible after the surgery.

We arrive at the hospital and head for admissions. For some reason, I'm not in a panic, and I prove that by remembering not only my name but also why I'm there when the clerk asks. We're directed to pre-op, and thankfully, Lynn is allowed to stay with me until kickoff time. Not that she and I are chatting; rather, it's her physical presence that makes me feel secure. So she reads her iPad while I lie on the bed in my assigned cubicle, having changed into a surgical gown. We're waiting for something to happen.

Pre-op is a busy place, I notice, forgetting that I'd likely been here back in March. Serious-looking types dressed in green or pink scrubs are scooting back and forth, some holding clipboards, none talking to me so far. That is, until one of them strolls over while reading from her Notebook.

Without looking up, she says, "Mister … do you pronounce it Diamond?" Her accent sounds Russian, but I don't ask; this isn't a good time to provoke an international incident. Instead, I give her my sweetest smile since she must be an important cast member in my upcoming performance.

"Yup, that's me," I reply.

She looks down at her screen and then back up as if she's reading her lines. "I'm Dr. Zukov," she says. "I'll be in charge of your anesthesia during the surgery."

"All by yourself?" I ask. I must be getting nervous to ask such a dumb question. I can see Lynn's eyes rolling like mad, but surprisingly, she doesn't say anything.

"Oh no," says Dr. Zukov, who is smiling for the first time. "Dr. Jenny Lee will be there too. Both of us will take care of you."

A sudden erotic thought pops into my head, but I shake it off. "I just need to ask you a favor please."

Zukov has been typing furiously but stops. "Sure. What is it?"

"When we get to the OR, I don't want to know anything or feel anything. Just knock me out, okay?"

"Trust me," she says. "You won't have a clue."

As she starts to turn away, I say, "One more thing. When do you think I'll be going in?"

"In about an hour."

"Well, let's not dawdle. I have a Zumba class this afternoon."

Ever the wiseass, but under the circumstances, I'm allowed.

I'm being rolled down a hallway, and after numerous lefts and rights plus a quick elevator ride, my portable bed plows through a pair of swinging doors. My last thoughts are of Lynn holding my hand during most of the trip.

CHAPTER 6

OCTOBER 2015—SURGERY 2, WEEK 1

I wake up totally unsure of what day it is, what time it is, and what the hell is going on. Then I remember I've had the second round of surgery, which means it's over. That makes me practically ecstatic. Until I wonder if anything's wrong, which could mean it's *not* over, which definitely scares the crap out of me.

I want to ask Lynn if I'm okay, but I don't know where she is. Worse, I sense the breathing tube down my throat. It doesn't hurt, but calling out isn't in the cards right now. I'm frustrated—not that that matters—and I don't have the brainpower to figure anything out anyway. It's less work to just go back to sleep. So I do.

The next time I open my eyes, which is who knows when, Lynn is at my bedside looking down at me and smiling.

"You're okay. You did great."

Right on cue, tears pour out of me. I reach for her hand and grasp it tightly wishing I could tell her what I'm thinking. That I feel safe because I'm with her. That I'll get through this. And that I love her. I think she knows all of this, but just the same, I'd sure like to speak the words out loud. You'd think having been through this once before and only seven months ago I wouldn't be so emotional, but there you go.

I'm wondering if I'll recognize any of the ICU nurses from last time or if they'll remember me. Maybe it's better if they don't; there's no telling whom I may have cursed out, although realistically, odds are it was all of them.

That's when I hear some puttering around in my room. I see two nurses who appear to be from India or maybe Bangladesh. I'd like to find out when the breathing tube is coming out; it feels I was born with it. Since I can't ask verbally, I make a little noise by slapping my hand against one of the bed rails. One of the nurses is busy typing on the room's laptop on a wheeled cart while the other peeks over her shoulder. Satisfied with whatever is on the screen, she strolls out of the room. Neither has looked at me apparently not wanting to be bothered by the guy whose chest had been sawed in half a few days ago. *Were they so oblivious in ICU last time?* Probably not, but now that I think on it, there were a couple of nurses who were. Maybe these are they. *Great. Maybe I can write an apology.*

After a few dozen more rail slaps, Nurse I Don't Care reluctantly appears bedside. "Yes?" she asks, her annoyance with me quite obvious.

If I could reply, I'd say, *Thanks so much for asking while I'm still alive,* but since I can't, I just point at my mouth and shrug. Thankfully, she gets the question. Unfortunately, she answers me with a single word: "Later." *Gee, thanks for clearing that up.*

After what feels like a week but is probably just a few hours, both nurses have returned. "Ready to have that tube out?" asks one.

I nod furiously hoping it might just pop out. I'm remembering the last time I went through this. A pulmonary specialist with a nice smile stood bedside, said, "Ready, set, go," and pulled it out as smoothly as an angler reeling in an empty line. So I wasn't worried how this little procedure would feel. Too bad. I should have been. It took three or four attempts to withdraw it using some kind of device, and each time, it seemed to move up only a little. I gagged terribly thinking I was suffocating. But I decided to live if only to catch up with the two nurses some day and strangle them so they'd know how it felt.

Lynn is visiting. "Do you want to read?" she asks handing me my Kindle.

I'm still hoarse from the breathing tube, but at least my words can come out sounding as if I can still speak English. I fumble for the power switch, and the Patterson book I'd been in the middle of appears. Much as I'd like to get back to it, why would I waste any part of Lynn's visit by reading? So I tell her thanks, maybe later.

"Just read a few sentences out loud," she insists.

Now I get it. She wants to measure my with-it-ness. Thankfully, I haven't suffered any hallucinations to speak of—a couple of momentary visions but nothing like last time, which was a two-week visit to Woodstock. Still, even with my reading glasses on, I'm having trouble focusing.

"Okay" she says. "Let's try something else."

Lynn takes my Kindle and glasses, places them on the bed, and walks around to the other side. For the first time, I notice the wall to my left isn't made just of cinderblocks. It seems to be covered with something, but I'll be damned if I know what. Lynn stands between the bed and wall, and as I keep looking in that direction, I figure it out. There are at least a dozen extra-large copies of photographs taped together like a giant collage. Now

I'm straining to see the details. As I recognize one pic after another, my smile keeps widening.

"That's us at our wedding party," I say, proudly pointing to one photo in the middle.

"And where did we have it?" she asks.

I open my mouth, but nothing comes out. *How do I not know this?* It was only a little more than a year previously, but for the life of me I can't spit out the name of the restaurant. Which makes me feel like an idiot.

Lynn tries to coax it out of me. She obviously has more faith in me than I do. "Come on. The Bed ... the Bed ..."

Suddenly the dots connect. "The Bedford Post Inn!" I exclaim as if I'd just won Final Jeopardy.

We repeat this exercise with some other pictures, which at first are equally difficult to remember in detail. Though when it comes to those of our dogs, I pass with flying colors.

ICU is plenty boring when you're not delusional from medications, so I welcome almost any invasion of my personal space. Especially when the one doing the invading is my surgeon. I can't see him with the curtain at the end of my room drawn, but I know his voice. Of course, my last name has been spoken aloud, a clue that's hard to miss.

A moment later, the curtain is pulled aside, and there's Dr. Somerset with an assortment of resident groupies hanging on his every word. He looks at me but doesn't enter. I chuckle to myself wondering if aneurysms are contagious.

"You're doing great, Mr. Dymant," he says with a smile.

Predictably, the waterworks erupt. "This is the second time in a year you've saved my life," I choke out.

The doctor looks down at his feet. "You're very kind."

That's the exact phrase he used during a consultation we had back in July to discuss whether I was a candidate for a noninvasive aneurism repair, meaning no open-heart surgery. I wasn't that lucky, but the meeting was still worthwhile because I got to see what Somerset used to replace my aorta.

"We call it cabbage," he said, opening his desk drawer and removing what looked like a cross between a squid and a hot-water bottle.

"This is in me?" I asked impressed and weirded out.

"Yes it is."

"How long will it last?"

Somerset smiled. "Longer than you will."

We thanked him, but before leaving, I told him we wouldn't be having this meeting were it not for him. Translation: *Thanks for saving my life the first time too.*

Since I do have some memories of the doting care I received in private ICU last time, never waiting more than a minute when I'd hit the Call button and no demeaning speaker grill to yell into, my goal is to stay in this unit for as long as possible. I figure that ought to shorten my time in the step-down ICU, which dispensed more trauma than pills. At least that's how I'm remembering it.

I've enlisted Lynn to help me strategize my campaign and have already done likewise with Dr. Silver, my cardiologist. I've even managed to persuade one ICU nurse using the "It would be in my best interest" argument. The way I see it, I had served a four-week sentence in this hospital back in March, so that should have earned me some points.

We make plans and God laughs. Just when I thought I had all my ICU ducks in a row, I hear a commotion outside my room. The curtain is pulled aside briefly, and Nurse Buddy, the one who's now in the "Let the poor guy stay here" camp, walks in frowning.

"What's wrong?" I ask her.

In a low voice, she says, "I can't believe it, but they're sending you to step-down."

Her words are like a punch in the gut. "When?"

"I don't know exactly, but today. Soon."

Before I can figure out what to throw that's breakable, a pair of white coats holding clipboards come into view. They're busy talking to each other, and my last name pops up. I don't think they'd notice me if my hair were on fire.

"Hey, excuse me!" I practically yell. I enjoy interrupting their conference; it makes me feel alive to wield such power. "What exactly's going on?"

Unfortunately, I don't get the salute I'm hoping for. In fact, I barely get any recognition at all. That is, until a few moments later one of them says, "Good news, Mr. Dymant. You're ready to leave ICU."

I decide right then and there not to give up without a fight. "Oh really?" I bark. "I don't think so. Last time, I was sent to step-down too soon, and they had to return me here." I give him my sweetest, phoniest smile. "You don't want that to happen again, *do you?*" I emphasize the last two words as if he'd be so intimidated by that that he'd apologize and come tuck me in. Fat chance.

"Well, we need the bed for a patient coming in, and you're the healthiest patient on this ward."

I immediately think, *That's not saying much. What this is really about is filling the ICU bed. In other words—ka-ching!* Unfortunately for me, no insight on my part is going to delay my resettlement, so I'll have to save my story for *60 Minutes*.

Their discussion over, Nurse Buddy turns to me. "I'm sorry. For what it's worth, I think you should stay longer too."

In a last act of desperation, I ask her to call Lynn and let her know what's happening. Turns out she already has. "Your wife was pretty upset," she says, glancing at the wall clock behind me. "She'll be here later."

I'm truly impressed with Nurse Buddy's dedication and think maybe they should promote her to hospital president.

The subject is quickly changed as she informs me that the drainage tube, the one lodged in my chest, has to come out. I wasn't even aware it was in, and the image suddenly makes me feel woozy. It's a good thing I'm lying down. "It's a little yucky, but it takes only a sec," she says, sounding like a teenager. She closes with, "Then we'll get rid of the catheter, and you'll be good to go. You've had one before, right?"

Oh yes, and I had it out. Then back in and out a second time. Just hold a pillow over my face until I flatline, okay?

Fortunately, both "procedures" go off without a hitch and I survive. Minutes later, the curtain is pulled aside by an orderly. *They really want this bed.*

"Hold on," I say to my nurse, who's gathering my few belongings and placing them in a plastic bin. I point at the wall to my left. "I'm not going anywhere without my photographs."

I can really kick ass when properly motivated. With surgical precision, she peels them away from the cinderblock in groups, and with no other place to put them, she begins to lay them on top of me. By the time she's done, I'm wearing them like a sheet. As orderlies front and rear wheel me out of the ICU and toward the elevators, I'm thinking of how to use my appearance for comic relief. The answer comes fast enough. "Nice," says a young-looking guy in green scrubs eyeballing my outfit as we wait for the elevator doors to open. I look over at him and smile.

"Like it? I got matching pillowcases at home."

The ride to my step-down room takes only a few minutes, not that I'm in a hurry to get there. As far as I'm concerned, we can do a few laps around the parking lot and then visit the cafeteria for coffee and a danish—anything to postpone depositing me in a room on that ward. Of course I've no chance of scoring with either idea, so I just accept reality.

We exit the elevator and head down the hall. We come to a stop, and the two orderlies begin the near-impossible task of maneuvering a seven-foot-long bed through a four-foot-wide entrance. I've no idea what subject the person who designed this room majored in, but it wasn't physics. After collisions with the doorjambs, we finally get in.

The first thing I notice is that the near bed is occupied, which must mean I've been assigned the one by the window! This is no doubt mere luck though I prefer to believe the powers that be have simply caved to my irresistible charm and influence.

As we creep along, I notice a young woman seated near the patient's bed reading a book. I say hello in their general direction, let the orderlies get me and my bed into position, and take the bin with my Kindle and multiple pairs of glasses I'm handed. They leave.

My first goal is to make friends with my roommate. This strategy for mental survival worked very well last time—I went through three of them—so I immediately repeat my greeting and this time add my first name. The lack of any reply friendly or otherwise doesn't dissuade me; I just assume he's asleep, so I turn my attention to his visitor.

"Are you the daughter?" I ask.

"No" she answers. "I'm an aide."

"Oh I see." Actually, I don't see. I'm confused having been under the impression that a hospital patient couldn't hire a private aide. But if I'm wrong, and apparently I must be, then why don't I do likewise? Excited, I tell her I'm interested in the service, could I get a business card with their number. I learn that no, they work only with patients who are members of a certain medical group. This isn't computing in my non-dot-connecting brain very well, so I'm having trouble explaining it to Lynn on the phone. She'll come see me later in the day, but I don't want to wait.

"So why can't you hire someone from her company?" she asks for what feels like the tenth time and probably is since I still don't get it myself.

Then an idea strikes me, which will probably exhaust my IQ for the rest of the day. "When is, what's his name, you know, the aide, when is he supposed to start at the house?"

Lynn was so exhausted running back and forth between home and hospital for a month last time that it was a miracle she didn't become a patient here. In fact, she had it even harder once I got home nursing me on her own until I could start to care for myself. We weren't about to press our luck a second time, so through an acquaintance of hers who ran a placement service, we hired a nice fellow from Ghana to help out for a month or two after my discharge.

"His name is Andrew, remember?" says Lynn sounding a bit exasperated. She's having a tough time keeping patient with my lack of recall. So am I.

"Right. Andrew. I forgot. Any reason why he can't start right away, like tomorrow? I mean here at the hospital."

I can almost see Lynn smile. I know she likes this idea almost as much as I do. "I'll call the agency first thing in the morning," she says. "But I don't see why not unless he got another job. Aides don't make any money if they're not working you know."

Fortunately, that doesn't happen. Lynn calls me right after breakfast to announce that yes Andrew is still available to start whenever we want. So he'll show up the following day at ten and leave at six for seven days a week and keep it going when I get home. I'm beginning to feel like royalty. Of course if I were, I wouldn't have to pay for this. But still … *Wow. My own personal aide? Things are looking up!*

CHAPTER 7

SURGERY 2, WEEK 2

"It is you! I heard you were back! How are you?"

I'm looking at the day nurse who's just come on shift and haven't a clue who she is. But she's making me feel like a celebrity with all her enthusiasm, so I figure I'll play along. "Hi," I say politely.

She writes her name along with today's aide on the board across from my bed as I fumble around looking for my distance glasses. If I can find them quickly enough, I'll be able to read her name and won't have to admit I've forgotten it. Too late.

"You don't remember me?" she asks, turning around with a pout, more statement than question. "It's Diane."

Somehow, the name and the face come together as do the memories of the care she gave me back in March. Diane was far and away my favorite nurse, and as I recall just that, I break into a smile and so does she. It's a huggable moment, but there's too much risk of pulling out a wire or tube, so we just beam at each other from a safe distance.

This begins a series of reunions over the next few days between me, the former and now repeat patient, and a variety of nurses and aides who took care of me during round 1 and were for the most part attentive and just plain likeable. As one after the other regrets me, I wonder if I truly appreciated them as much as I hope I did. After all, I was still delusional, agitated, crabby, and miserable by the time I reached step-down and had been no doubt a real joy to deal with. So now I'm wondering whether to start apologizing to anyone who says he or she remembers me or just play dumb. I decide dumb is the way to go. After all, maybe they've forgotten my rantings, so why remind them?

One white coat who comes into my room claiming to have seen me before turns out to be someone I'd just as soon forget.

"Mister … umm … Dymant?" he asks.

Why do they always state your name in question form? Who else could I be? "No, I'm George Bush." He's standing close enough for me to read the name badge. Dr. Toliver looks to be about my age but with half as much hair. The words Infectious Disease are embroidered on his breast pocket. I'm wondering what this guy wants. I'm also wondering how it feels to walk around with a moniker like that. It gives me the chills.

Toliver reaches out to shake hands, so I guess there's no risk of catching something. He takes a quick glance at the clipboard he's carrying, and then the reason for his visit is clear—there isn't one. "I just wanted to let you know that you don't have any infections," he says with a little grin. This news isn't news at all.

"I know I don't, otherwise, I'd be running a fever and my white counts would be elevated," I reply with a grin of my own. The good doctor is learning that I'm not a complete ignoramus, but he isn't budging. He wants to bill this "consultation" no matter what.

"Ahh, but you did have a fever back in ICU. A hundred and three as I recall."

I fold my arms across my chest just to show him I mean business. "You must have me confused with another patient. If I'd been running a fever that high, my wife would've told me."

Toliver feel the glands under my jaw, pronounces me fit as a fiddle, and leaves. He'll bill Oxford, my insurance company, but I sure showed him. Which reminds me—the first surgery and monthlong stay cost well over $1 million, but thanks to the high-end coverage I have, my out-of-pocket expenses were manageable. I wonder how much this one will run—half a million? More? And how does a patient without top-notch insurance pay for it?

I intercept the buck-toothed, tuxedoed (yes, he's actually wearing a faux tuxedo) waiter when I hear him asking my roommate what he'd like for lunch. Since I haven't had any real food in what feels like a month, my appetite is now on par with that of a jungle animal. Raw carcasses don't appeal to me, but the thought of a double cheeseburger sure does. I'm remembering that this heart-unhealthy entrée was somehow available to me last time, so unless the menu's changed, I'm going to order it again.

As it turns out, the bad news is they don't have it. Worse, they haven't taken me off my liquid diet yet, which means there's no point asking what else there is to eat since I'll be getting another tray of ice cream, lemon ices, and Jell-O. I can't hear myself think over the noises my stomach is making. I make plans to bombard the next medical person I see with a demand for calories. I won't take out my frustration on the waiter, though; he's not the guy who can lift the carbs embargo anyway. Ordinarily, I wouldn't be very patient waiting for a white coat to appear, but with real food at stake, I know it's just a matter of time.

"First you need to pass a swallow test."

Such is the condition for a ordering a cheeseburger or any other member of the protein universe according to the physician's assistant who finally shows up bedside twenty minutes after I ask for one.

"What exactly is that?" I ask nearly laughing. Swallow? How do they think I've been making the ice cream disappear—by stashing it under my bed? My drive for meaningful sustenance is greater than my desire to argue, so I play along when the two "specialists" in charge of the "exam" show up that afternoon. One hands me a cup of water. I think she's the one running this show. The other takes a seat against the wall notebook in hand.

"All right, Mr. Dymant," says the water bearer. "I want you to take three gulps in a row and then say your name out loud."

If I already had a mouthful of water, I would've probably spit it out. "Are you joking?"

She gives me a serious look, so I dutifully perform as requested enunciating each syllable of my name just to remove any doubt about my swallowing ability. As they prepare to leave, I wonder, *Why did this test require two people considering the one with the notebook's only job was to enter the "test" results?* Answer—two bills to Oxford are better than one.

I must say the quality of service I'm getting in step-down this time around feels altogether different from how it was in March; even the aides seems downright cheerful by comparison. That might be due to my new friend, Andrew, handling some of the chores I'd ordinarily bother them with. Or maybe someone read them the riot act and they're afraid Lynn will file another complaint if they give her a reason to. I can't think of any other possibility though in truth it just might be because my overall attitude seems to have changed. Having been through the grinder once before, I think I know pretty much what to expect, and that experience has transformed me into a patient who's a little less afraid and belligerent and therefore a little calmer and saner. *Little* being the operative word here.

Even an unplanned development doesn't completely throw me for a loop, at least not to the extent it did back then. I was still in my delusional and paranoid state in step-down when I was informed that the port in my neck needed to be changed. Somehow, this was the chosen location for delivering meds in a hurry, not that I understood why the IV couldn't handle it. But I didn't give it much thought since I'd woken up with the port in recovery. Unfortunately, its life span was limited, and medical tape was no longer keeping it in place, so I was told I needed it replaced. I had no idea what this entailed until the next thing I knew, a surgeon and nurse came into my room, closed the curtain, covered me with some sort of tarp from head to toe, and gave new meaning to the word *torture*. Barely a word of explanation was offered, and I was absolutely terrified throughout the hour-long ordeal.

I was subjected to a repeat performance of this assault less than a week later, and though a different surgeon and nurse team handled it sympathetically, my earlier trauma was too fresh to ignore. Despite their best efforts, it was just as scary and equally painful.

So given my poor track record for taking unscheduled medical procedures in stride, it's remarkable to me that I can keep my cool when a nurse practitioner tells me I need a chest tube, the type that had been removed just before I left ICU, put back in. Well, maybe I'm not cool, but at least I'm not trying to climb out the window. Since I need to feel in control in situations like this, my first reaction is to cross-examine the witness. "Why?" I ask. "Was it taken out by mistake? If so, who's mistake was it?"

She calmly replies that it's needed; they don't want fluids building up, and no, it wasn't taken out by mistake.

"Well, all right," I say, conceding defeat. "Since I need it."

As I'm handed a consent form to sign, she informs me that this maneuver will require a little trip to the radiology OR. "And how long will this take?" I ask cringing.

"Oh, I'd say thirty minutes or so."

Now that's an opening I can't resist. "Oh come on. It'll take that long just to get my bed out of the room."

An orderly comes for me that afternoon. Since Lynn is aware I've passed the swallow test, I'm confident she'll bring me something mouthwatering to eat at the end of the day. Maybe brisket or mac & cheese; I'm betting the types of food she'd ordinarily frown on are on the shopping list. I'm picturing a rack of lamb, but the image goes poof as I'm wheeled into the OR. Three characters in scrubs and masks greet me with hellos and little waves. They could be smiling, but I can't tell. Two of them carefully move me from the hospital bed to the table and quickly cover me with a blanket when they notice I'm shivering.

"Thanks," I say. "It's like a meat locker in here."

I don't realize the gallows-humor pun at first, but the laughs all around give it away.

Turns out the NP's thirty-minute estimate wasn't so far off the mark, and when I get back to my room, Andrew tells me I've been gone an hour, maybe less. He also points out that all my electronic devices—cell phone, Kindle, Notebook—are being charged. That makes me happy since they're my chief means of entertainment and link to the outside world.

With my chest implant (no, not that kind of implant) out of the way, I plan my evening activities beginning with dinner while Lynn visits. After she leaves, I'll check email, maybe try to write one or two. Then a Netflix movie, something silly like *Police Squad* with Leslie Nielsen. And before I nod off for the night, text, "Sweet dreams, love you" to Lynn.

My roommate has been moved to some other ward. I've learned the poor guy was having breathing problems. Since we never spoke, I didn't know what his condition was other than being cardiac related. His replacement hasn't been especially chatty either, though that's because he's spending a lot of time on his cell phone talking with a variety of people. Since he's here, which means he's had major cardiac surgery, I'm shocked to overhear him demanding the fattiest foods possible multiple times a day from whomever he talks to. He even insists on trying to get to the cafeteria.

"I'm sure they've got corned beef or something," he explains to the other party who is apparently resisting his deli order.

The guy looks a lot older than me, weighs as much as a grand piano, and is a sure bet to boomerang back a week after he goes home assuming he lives that long. For me, once I'm discharged, I'll do whatever it takes to stay the hell out of here. I'll come back for CT scans and checkups, but in-patient? Thanks but no thanks.

It seems I have a talent for atrial fibrillations or a-fibs for short, a condition in which the heart rate isn't just irregular; it can fly right off the charts and raise the possibility of a stroke or worse. It happened to me after the first surgery last March and again this time, not that I was aware of it since I was out cold. Hence my surprise when Lynn gives me a quick summary of the most recent events.

"They needed to zap you a couple of times," she says.

"You're kidding," I say, trying to comprehend this. "You mean with the paddles to the chest and yelling 'Clear!'?"

She shakes her head. "That's not how they do it nowadays. It's more like panels they place on you."

Oh how stylish.

The multiple zapping means I must have a-fibbed more than once, and that's disturbing. Even more so is that it happens again during my second day in step-down. Naturally, this causes a near panic among the white coats and rightfully so. My heart rate has clocked in at a breathtaking 160, and if it's not brought down quickly, I might explode like the *Hindenburg*. Fortunately, it's back under control once I lie still and some meds are pumped into me through the IV. That was a close one, I guess.

I've now learned another medical term—sinus rhythm—which has nothing to do with breathing through my nose. Rather, it's the steadiness of my heart rate and my body's ability to keep it within a normal range. Now that I know what it means, I can't wait to use it in a sentence, and my first chance comes soon enough.

"Hello, Mr. Dymant," says the perky physician's assistant as she strolls into my room. I know her; she's a nice one, so I give her a "Hi" returning as much perkiness as I can muster and then follow it with, "What's up?"

"Oh, not much. Just checking your meds. Oh by the way, someone from cardiology might stop by later to discuss Coumadin with you, you know, the blood thinner?"

The very word is making the hairs on my neck stand up. My first wife, Susie, who died of uterine cancer at the too-young age of fifty-four, was prescribed that med to help control a dangerous clot in her leg. Problem was no one mentioned how often the drug's level in her bloodstream needed to be checked. That is, until I found her passed out in our bathroom and an ambulance had to rush her to the ER. When I told Lynn the story, she mentioned that the same thing happened to her late father in a movie theater.

Sufficiently armed with these vignettes, I waste no time sharing my point of view with the PA. "It'll be a short discussion I can tell you that," I say, all my perkiness now vanished. I proceed to recap Susie's and Lynn's father's experiences with Coumadin, and before she can comment, I close with an instruction. "Besides, I've been in sinus rhythm for what, two days straight? So just write, 'Won't take Coumadin' in my chart."

Much to my surprise and relief, the PA simply nods, smiles, and walks out of the room. I mentally file this incident under Patient Victories and try to remember what I've ordered for dinner. Not a cheeseburger. Probably chicken.

Later that evening, after Andrew and Lynn have gone, the night nurse comes into my room. She's middle-aged, short, and cheerless. Lasering my wristband as required before dispensing any meds to a patient, she asks me my name and if I know where I am. It's tempting to answer Babe Ruth and Yankee Stadium just to see how she'll react, but I'm afraid she'll think I'm serious and offer me antipsychotics. So I reply like the relatively clearheaded person I am and swallow each pill after she recites its name and purpose. When she comes to the last one, however, all hell breaks loose and that's because it's Coumadin. I practically leap out of the bed. "What the …?"

It's all I can do not to strangle her, but I assault her verbally. "Didn't you check my goddamned file? It's supposed to indicate that I won't take this drug. So the question is why the hell are you trying to give it to me?"

She tries to calm me down using nonsensical techniques like reason and logic, but I'm not having any of it. "Look. I have the right to refuse any drug I wish. You know that, right?"

She nods looking a bit worried. How she'll explain this patient rebellion to her superiors is not my problem.

"Do you know why it was prescribed?" she asks making another attempt to get through to me. "Becau—"

I cut her off at the knees. "Yeah, yeah, I know. It's because I a-fibbed, but that was two days ago, and I've been steady ever since, so—" I cut myself off. "Tell me, who exactly prescribed the Coumadin?"

She walks over to the laptop on wheels and takes a look. "Dr. Anderson," she says.

I remember this guy. He was one of my surgeons last March, though I don't think he worked on me this time. I also recall him telling me in ICU to keep using the breathing toy since I had a collapsed lung. In fact, that wasn't my condition, but he nearly scared me to death. Some bedside manner, and now he's trying to slip me a drug I don't want?

I give the nurse my deadliest laser-beam stare. "Listen, Anderson isn't my attending. You tell him the only doctors I'll discuss medications with are Somerset or Margolis, no one else. Are we clear on this?"

Realizing any further debate would be pointless, she slinks away defeated. Now I'm wide awake and could use a sleep aid, but the last thing I want is to see that nurse again, so I distract myself with another movie on Netflix.

My surgeon pops in for a visit the next morning and says he has no problem dropping the Coumadin recommendation—another win for me—but he warns that he'll be pushing it if I a-fib again. Fair enough.

Visitors help me pass the time. Lynn stops by at the end of each day dinner in hand, and it's a lot better than what the buck-toothed waiter serves. I have to admit, though, there's been a marked improvement in one category since March—they get the order right more often.

There's the usual assortment of blood drawers and x-ray takers, and I try to schmooze with them. Dr. Mehdi from cardiology stops by every morning to check on me after which he reports to my local equivalent, who's not affiliated with this hospital. He's a decent sort, warm, and rather low key. One time, he floors me by asking how my spirits are instead of posing the typical check-the-box questions. I ask him why he didn't become a psychotherapist because he seems to have a gift for it.

My daughter shows up during her lunch break a few times with turkey wraps for me and salads for herself. She's surprisingly upbeat, which allows us to joke around. That's become easier since it seems likely I'll survive. Seth, my office assistant, calls me ahead of his visits to take my order from the food court though we both know what I always want—black coffee and a cheese danish. Andrew the aide politely heads for the cafeteria when any friend or family member stops by. Otherwise, he's a constant presence until the evening, when he goes home. We're getting along fine now that I've gotten used to his accent and developed some patience with his limited command of colloquial English. It's a good thing too since he'll be helping me for at least another month once I get home. Overall, he's proven reliable, friendly, and dedicated. There's no task beneath him it seems, and I'm lucky to have him.

Not everyone I'd like to see show up actually does, however. Susan, my therapist, can't though she texts me words of encouragement that make me smile. Susan played such an integral role in my getting emotionally ready for this surgery; I can't imagine what shape I would have been in without her.

Diane, my other therapist—massage in her case—wants to visit but has been recovering from a virus she picked up from one of her three little children. So we FaceTime instead like the friends we really are, and though a foot rub would be nice, this feels just as good, maybe better.

My favorite nurse, the one with the same name, pops in to replace an IV bag during our live chat, so I quickly make introductions. "Diane, this is Diane," I say, turning my iPhone back and forth between them. It feels nice to be surrounded by such caring souls as these.

This hospital must have a psychiatric ward because the voice just outside my room sounds like it belongs to one of their patients, one who should be back in a padded room. He's loud and angry, ranting and cursing about some procedure that was supposedly bungled. My roommate, the oversized one with a penchant for pastrami, has been discharged, and amazingly, no one has taken his place yet. It's late at night, and I'm totally alone in the dark while this is going on. It's making me feel very uneasy, so I fumble for the remote and press the Call button. I'd like to request a SWAT team, but I'll settle for just about anyone they send.

A few minutes later, one of the aides I know walks in. "What's up?" he asks. He's a big, burly sort, and considering it's suddenly become quiet in the hall, I wonder if he simply body-slammed the crazy guy. But it's not quiet for long as the maniacal voice returns.

"I'll get me a gun and shoot everyone! That's what I'll do!" the crazed man yells. "The goddamned doctors! Yeah, and the patients too!"

The aide and I exchange a look, and I point at the door. "What's up? *That's* what's up!" I reply in a panicky voice. "Isn't there security here? What about the cops? Something!"

The aide doesn't appear concerned as if threats of mass murder happen here all the time. "Don't worry," he says. "I'll just close your door on the way out."

Considering this guy can bench-press my car, I was hoping for a slightly more aggressive strategy, for example, putting the nut in a sleeper hold. Instead, for the next half hour, I listen to exchanges between the patient and what sounds like a pair of doctors trying to calm him down. At this point, I'm the one who needs to be calmed down. My heart is pounding; I'm breathing shallow and fast. I'm in true fight-or-flight mode, but unfortunately, I'm in no position to do either. I thought I'd made progress since my first surgery, but I still feel vulnerable as all hell. The commotion in the hall has disappeared, but I'm still shook up. I don't sleep a wink that night.

Diane the nurse is back the next morning, and I can barely acknowledge her—that's how exhausted I am from the sleepless night before. "Hi, Diane," I mumble.

She whirls around hands on hips. "You know," she says, trying to keep a straight face, "I was going to disconnect some of your lines since you don't need them anymore. But if you'd rather keep them, I can just go."

She's such a card. I hide my poker face as best I can and fake whining. "Well, you're already here, so I guess you can take them."

We crack up laughing, but when Diane settles down, I can sense something's wrong. Burnout. "You all right?" I ask her. She's been beyond good to me, and I really care about her.

Diane shakes her head. "Not really," she says. "Yesterday, I had to deal with this crazy patient up until my shift ended."

I sit up straight as an arrow. "Yikes! The guy who wanted to shoot everyone? *That guy?*"

Her shake turns into a nod. "Yup, that guy. And we were shorthanded too, so I had to deal with it by myself."

Now I'm the one shaking my head. We spend the next few minutes exchanging our respective war stories when I decide to change tack.

"What time do you get off today?" I ask.

Diane's hands go right back to her hips. "Why? Are you asking me out?"

"No, dummy. You know I'm married, and so are you."

That produces a grin. Obviously, my irresistible charm is working. "What I'm getting at is you should do something just for yourself after work. Open a bottle of wine, cook a gourmet meal with your husband, get a massage. Believe me, you'll forget all about yesterday."

Diane's smile has been widening all throughout my little pep talk. "You know what I like about you, Michael?" she asks.

"Well, it's a long list I'm sure. Just give me your top three."

"Now who's the dummy? It's simple. You get me."

I smile back and think, *Isn't that what everyone wants?*

Lynn tells me I've been here twelve days, which compared to last time isn't so very long. But I must be making progress since the number of tubes and wires that connect me to modern science keeps shrinking. At least I think it is. Even though my anesthesia party ran for only half as long as last time, seven or eight hours lying unconscious with a brain full of drugs still creates quite a drag on cognition. So while I know I'm moving along, it's not so much by remembering what I'm no longer attached to. Instead, it's by focusing on what the nurses tell me I still need to keep plugged in. Make no mistake—one thing I do know is the less crowded my IV pole is, the closer I am to leaving this joint.

"And when does the battery pack go?" I ask a friendly PA who stops in for a quick check of my surgical wounds and latest vitals.

"Oh, we'll keep that humming until the last day."

The device, a small yet heavy box with leads running in and out, is insurance in case my heart decides to breakdance. It has wires running directly to my heart, the image of which makes me feel faint. Worse is recalling that they're literally yanked out as one of my roommates last March experienced. He was cursing early and often. I'm suddenly not in a rush to go home.

CHAPTER 8

EXIT

An unfamiliar person strolls into my room on a Thursday morning with clipboard in hand. She's wearing civvies, so I cleverly rule out nurse, doctor, or any other medical-type person. Maybe she's the president of the hospital and wants to thank me for the truckloads of cash Oxford has paid them on my behalf this year. Or maybe she's *from* Oxford and wants to strangle me for the same reason.

She identifies herself as the resident discharge social worker, and at the sound of her title, I can feels the blood pumping through my synthetic aorta. Back in the spring, it seemed I'd never get home. My release was tied to an exam by the head of ophthalmology and neurology about my blurred vision. He came to the hospital only once a week, and I couldn't see him until I was no longer attached to an IV. Talk about a catch-22.

This time, I don't have any such condition for leaving other than the standard list—no infections, a bladder that empties, and suitable home care.

My one-woman parole board glances at her clipboard and without looking up asks, "Mr. Dymant?" She's asking the obvious, so I'm sure she fits in perfectly around here.

"That's what they call me," I reply. Her chuckle tells me there's an actual sense of humor under her bureaucratic exterior, not exactly a plentiful commodity on this ward. Margaret runs through a checklist of questions that center mostly on how I'll manage after I've been sprung. "Like last time," I say and glance at Andrew, my aide. "But with a lot more help. And for as long as I need it."

Margaret is practically overjoyed on hearing this, and I don't think she's overdoing it. Back in March, one of my roommates who had the same surgery I did tried to persuade his discharge social worker that he'd manage fine alone in his house thanks to a brother "who's only an hour away." She left our room shaking her head even more than I was.

"You can't expect them to let you go without support at home," I called out in his general direction. "Otherwise, they'll send you to in-patient rehab. If you want to go home, set up enough home care so she won't panic and you won't fall down the stairs."

He walked out of the room a few days later, the brother on one side and his ex-wife on the other. He smiled at me and said one of them was moving in.

I snap out of my daydream and return to the present. "So Margaret, any departure date I should know about?" I'm practically salivating as she consults the all-knowing clipboard.

"I'm told it's Saturday or Sunday" is her reply, and with that, she glides out of the room.

"Great news!" Andrew exclaims handing me my cell phone. He knows I want to tell Lynn right away. Yet even as I speed-dial her number, my stomach begins to twist into knots. How do I know Margaret knows what she's talking about? Hospitals won't discharge patients from step-down ICU on weekends. *Didn't I hear that somewhere?* Then again, why would she be so specific about my release if she didn't know when it would be? And she did say she was told when. She wouldn't just make it up, would she? I really should keep this internal debate to myself but can't. Instead, I immediately blather it into the phone as soon as Lynn picks up. Fortunately, she quickly interrupts me, which forces me to take a breath; otherwise, I might pass out from lack of oxygen.

"Michael, stop! Whether you go home Sunday or Monday doesn't matter. What counts is that you'll be out of there soon."

Ahh, the voice of reason.

Soon is right. While no one gives me a sworn statement, the consensus among the white coats is that I'll be going home Monday. Armed with this information, I breeze through the weekend watching movies on Netflix and comedy specials on YouTube and reading Patterson on my Kindle. I'm still without a roommate, which leads me to believe I either have intolerable body odor or the hospital treats returning surgical patients like the celebrities we are. Since no one's run out of my room holding his or her nose, I decide it's my star status that explains my luxury suite.

Lynn takes the weekend off from visiting, and I'm okay with that; she really needs some me time. Besides, I still have the hovering Andrew at my side each day. He can't bring me dinner, but we do have some interesting discussions over lunch on subjects ranging from politics to the economy.

My excitement over the prospect of being discharged keeps me up at night, but rather than asking for a sleep aid, I choose instead to schmooze with the nurse on late shift for the weekend. We remember each other from last March and share an interest in all things metaphysical.

"You've survived for a reason," Marie says to me at one point. "You just don't know what that reason is yet. But some day you will."

I nod in agreement since I'm too choked up to speak.

Monday morning arrives as does Andrew at eight sharp. He's not carrying a newspaper, especially the one I'd like to see with a front-page headline that reads "Michael Dymant Discharged This Morning!" So on a leap of faith, I ask him to begin packing my overnight bag, the one I checked in with. That is, until I realize that all there is to pack are my toiletries, electronic gadgets, and extra pajamas. "Let's wait until we're closer to my going home," I say.

We sit and wait for something to happen.

Less than hour later, which is pretty quick in hospital time, Dr. Margolis, my surgical team's second in command, appears in the doorway of my room with a perky nurse standing next to him. He reads through some paperwork, and they exchange a few whispered comments that I strain to hear but can't.

Suddenly, Margolis looks my way and smiles. "Well, Mr. Dymant, I'd say you're ready to go home today. How does that sound?"

Back in March, I wanted to deck this guy. Now, I could kiss him. I sit up and practically salute just to show him how ready I am.

"Just disconnect my wires and point me to the exit," I reply.

He leans over to the nurse and whispers again, though this time, I can hear what he's saying.

"You know, he has a completely different attitude this time."

I practically laugh out loud. It helps when you're out in two weeks instead of a month. They smile, and I receive a little good-luck wave from them.

I give Lynn the news but can't be specific about the time since no one has given me a clue yet. She's not happy about that though she understands since we just went through this in April.

A nurse stops by a little while later to inform me that my labs and urine are "just great," and she disconnects my battery pack. The act of yanking out the wires from my chest turns out to be a painless nonevent since all I can focus on is being another step closer to going home.

I eat lunch without tasting anything, but that's not difficult since it's rather tasteless. I won't miss having meals here. After my tray is collected, the discharge nurse enters. She frowns and carries the demeanor of the grade-school teacher you didn't want.

"Let's review your discharge instructions," she says stiffly, no doubt counting the days until retirement. She consults my file: first CT scan, first appointment with surgeon's NP, first appointment with cardiologist. I've decided to switch to Dr. Mehdi, the one who asked about my spirits, but I get the feeling there's no reason to tell her that. She continues as if reading from a script, which of course she is. I'm to watch my blood pressure. I'm to watch my weight.

"In case I gain or lose?" I quip.

Nurse Frown looks at me like a dog who just peed on her shoe. Plenty of people here are allergic to penicillin and I get the nurse who's allergic to puns.

"I'm serious," she says, a given since she doesn't appear to have a nonserious side. "And no lifting more than ten pounds. Otherwise, you could split wide open."

Now she has my full attention. I shiver as I sign the document and wonder how much my overnight bag weighs.

There are no other regulatory requirements left, so I've changed into workout clothes but not because I'll be going to the gym anytime soon. Since I'm packed and ready to leave, I give Lynn the update, which is a little less vague this time as all that stands between me and the exit is a wheelchair. I'd like to skip the transportation but know better. I don't have a lot of stamina yet, and the building would probably go into lockdown if I tried it.

"It won't take long, so I'll leave now," Lynn says.

I hope she's right since I'd really like to get out of here. "Okay," I reply. "I'll ask for the chair and text you when I'm rolling."

The ETA for the wheelchair is "As soon as there's one available," so I decide to pass the time by slow-walking down the hall. As I do, memories of the dozens of such trips this past year come flooding back. With the physical or occupational therapist after breakfast. With Seth after a danish. With Lynn after dinner. By myself even though I struggled. The feeling of euphoria that came from being mobile.

I pass by other patients' rooms as I make my way. I've no idea who any of the occupants are or what shape they're in; still, I feel like yelling, "See? I'm going home, and so will you! And I've done it twice!" I keep my thoughts to myself, and after reaching the lounge, I do a U-turn and head to the nurses' station. I'm hoping to see my favorite nurse, Diane, but she's not around, so I settle for a few smiles and unenthusiastic good lucks. I'm fresh out of time-killing ideas, so I head back to my room.

Andrew has carefully removed the blown-up photos that were taped to the blinds, and they now sit in a neat stack on the bed next to my overnight bag and discharge folder. "Thanks," I say to him. "You haven't seen a wheelchair go by, have you?"

Of course he can't tell I'm kidding and practically bolts out of the room to look for it. I'm telling him not to bother when as if on cue an orderly pushes one up to the doorway, spins it around, and announces my name.

"That's me," I say joyously.

Calling seems faster than texting even though it isn't, so I get off the bed and speed-dial Lynn. "The wheelchair just showed up," I say.

"I'm double parked in front of the building" is her instant comeback. "Move your butt!"

It takes me a minute or two to walk to the doorway, do an about-face, and ease myself into the wheelchair since I'm not yet in move-your-butt mode. Andrew places my belongings in my lap, the orderly pulls me out into the hall, and we head for the elevators. We pass a few white coats and green scrubs along the way all of whom totally ignore me. For once I don't really mind. I'm going home!

EPILOGUE

JUNE 2016—A SAD FAREWELL

The digital readout on my SUV's dashboard reads one forty-five. If I'm on time, I'll make it to my last session with Susan in fifteen minutes. I've been driving to her office myself for the past three months, and it's been uneventful other than those times when it's rained, in which case it was harder for me to see clearly. Unfortunately, my vision isn't any better fifteen months after the ministroke that took place during my first surgery in March 2015, and it's not likely to improve in the future, but that's not much of an issue on this sunny and warm June day.

Though I've already been here a dozen times, I still like to use the GPS just to hear the voice say, "Your destination will be on the left in nine hundred feet." At the sound of that announcement, I get ready to pull into her building's parking lot. The entire long block is a series of old yet nicely kept homes that were converted into multioffice dwellings mostly occupied by social workers and psychologists. Birds of a feather I suppose.

I find a space in the lot behind the building, turn off the engine, look to my right, and sigh. Lynn told me that orchids were Susan's favorite, so I picked some up at a garden center on the way as a thank-you and happy retirement gift. Hard to believe this is my final session with Susan. I could use a hundred more.

We clicked on that very first day thirteen months ago when she came to our house, and the intensity just took off and never stopped growing. More often than not, I'd be so exhausted after two hours of soul-searching and tears that I'd postpone feeding the dogs and collapse in a heap on the couch instead. But I'd still find the energy to send her a text to say how much each session meant to me. I was pretty sure she always knew that, but I'd send it anyway.

I walk around to the other side of the car, carefully take out the potted orchid, and head for the back entrance of the building. Once inside, I quickly spot the water cooler and realize I didn't bring a bottle from home. Oh well, just what I need is to carry a large cupful up two flights of stairs and then drop the plant. *Forget that. I'll get some after the session is over.*

I reach the top of the stairs still impressed with my ability to climb them. I won't make the gymnastics team anytime soon, but I'm feeling rather Olympian compared to where I was a year ago. I'm halfway into a sitting position on one of the two chairs in the small waiting area when the door to Susan's office pops open. She smiles a greeting and turns around. I follow her inside.

"These are just beautiful! It was so considerate of you," she says, taking the flowers from me and carefully setting the bowl on a table.

I take my usual seat on the couch across from her. We look at each other for a few moments, both unsure where to begin. Well, at least I am. What do you say when it's the last session and there's so much more work to do?

"So," I say, tapping my fingers together, "I guess I can't guilt you out of this." When in doubt, make a dumb joke. Before Susan can answer, I put up a hand. "I'm kidding." She grins in response, and I add, "Well actually, I'm not."

Susan turns serious. "We've discussed my retirement as another in a series of losses for you."

"I know."

"Should we talk about it some more?"

I shake my head. "No, I don't think I need to. Unless of course *you* want to." Die-hard wiseass to the bitter end—that's me. "What I'd rather talk about it what I've learned from you this past year."

Hearing this, Susan looks about ready to throw confetti and take out noisemakers. She sits back in her chair like a triumphant teacher. "Go ahead. Tell me."

I'd been thinking about this ever since Susan announced her impending retirement three months earlier. "Well for starters, I've faced all of these terrifying events and survived. Which means I'm a lot stronger than I often give myself credit for."

Susan nods. "And you're more courageous too."

I smile, drop my head, and gaze at the floor. Compliments have always made me uncomfortable. Maybe someday I'll discover why. Looking back up, I continue. "So that means future medical events—and it's a good bet I'll have some—should be easier for me to face. At least I won't avoid them."

"Let's hope not," she says. "But that means more than major challenges like what you've been through. It also means how you care for yourself every day."

I nod along with her. "I know. Everything from annual physicals to how I eat to never smoking cigarettes again."

"How many years was that?"

"Forty-five."

"Wow," she says.

"Yeah," I say.

FINAL THOUGHTS

According to the American Heart Association, up to 25 percent of cardiac surgery patients suffer from depression while in the hospital and afterward. Add those who won't admit they're depressed and I'd say it's at least 50 percent.

When Susie, my first wife, was receiving chemo to treat her uterine cancer, she was visited by a Reiki practitioner, a social worker, and a music therapist. Even a guy with a golden retriever made the rounds. To say I was impressed with such emotional support would be an enormous understatement. I saw the impact of those visits etched on her face, and I was grateful for each one of them.

It was a totally different story on the cardiovascular ward where between my two surgical adventures I spent more than six weeks. While I did receive help from Andrew, my aide, my support network pretty much consisted of one person—Lynn. She advocated for me. She visited every day and usually twice. She delivered cards with inspirational messages and photographs from our wedding. She encouraged and reassured me. Grounded me. As I lay unconscious after my first surgery, a nurse told Lynn he was certain I'd be going home because I had her to go home to. He was right about that. But despite her efforts, I still experienced bouts of severe depression during, between, and after my stays in the hospital.

Research from organizations such as the Cleveland Clinic point to the link between depression and anxiety and cardiac surgery in that the former creates a more likely need for the latter. I believe there's a psychophysical connection between heart surgery and depression; not only is the body impacted, but it's as if the core of one's actual being has been assaulted. I have no reason to doubt this because when I look back, that's exactly how I felt.

The physical pain from my surgical wounds was severe, but in comparison to my spiritual and emotional suffering, they were more like paper cuts. And paradoxically, as those wounds healed a bit more each day, I felt increasingly vulnerable and powerless. A victim. I couldn't feel gratitude for being alive, only anger at the injustice of it all. That anger was then compounded by the recollection of every other trauma in my life. My brain was somehow building a case, compiling evidence to justify what I was going through. In short, I viewed this as the latest installment of my life story, one that was filled with loss and pain. That wasn't all there was to my life of course, but it was all I could see. It was the way I had come to define myself.

Now as I sit at my keyboard, it's clear to me that I no longer view my life that way. I'd spent years drawing a line from childhood to the present. Connecting parents who survived the Holocaust to having practically no extended family. To infertility and adoption. To leaving the family business. To the death of my first wife, my parents, and Lynn's mother. And finally to facing my own mortality. But I don't play the victim game anymore; it never produced anything useful in life. In fact, it was preventing me from *having* a life.

I've faced the past, I've come to understand and respect it, and it now remains where it belongs. Traumas I've experienced are no longer obstacles to my happiness. They are the life badges I've earned, the Medals of Honor I've bestowed on myself. And so therein lies the question I still ask myself from time to time: *How did I transition from victim to survivor?*

Before I try to answer that question, let me first reiterate one truth. I was lucky—no, blessed—to have Lynn help me cope. She did everything that one person could do for another. Not every patient is married, and even those who are don't always have someone as dedicated as my wife was to me. Though I needed more than what Lynn or any one person was capable of giving, the wind was always at my back because of her.

That said, my emotional growth has been an ongoing process, not a single event. I didn't just wake up one morning with a lightbulb shining over my head and being free of all the self-pity and victimization. There wasn't any aha moment. It's been a long, painful struggle, and I still have to work at it every day. Sometimes with success but not always. And while I do give myself credit for how far I've come, without help, I'd still be mired in the psychological quicksand of the past, recent and otherwise.

I'm sure you've realized from my journals that the help I received from Susan, my therapist, was critical to my evolving. So unless you're the poster child for emotional well-being—and really, who is?—a major piece of the puzzle for us patients is to pursue therapy. One evening in April when Lynn was visiting me in the step-down ICU, I was lucid enough to tell her that. "When I get home, I'm going to need to work with someone." Lynn just nodded her understanding. It was a far cry from what I'd told her when I was first admitted—"Haven't I been through enough already?"

88

Therapy comes in many flavors, as do therapists, so it's important to find the style that works for you and the practitioner with whom you have the right chemistry. Susan practiced a discipline called emotionally focused therapy, which stresses the role various emotions, such as anger, fear, and loss of trust, play in relationships. By extension, it can be an effective treatment for depression. She had worked alongside a chaplain on an oncology ward, and her love of poetry and Buddhism combined to produce just the right teacher for me, one who could understand and validate my feelings with compassion while opening doors for me with her extraordinary insight and knowledge.

Some years ago, I was struggling with another challenging period in my life. I found a nearby psychologist with evening hours, and after two months, I realized all he was doing was allowing me to storytell while offering nothing of value. Meanwhile, my wife (Susie at the time) was seeing someone else and raving about her. "You actually get written homework?" I asked her after coming home from yet another worthless session. "I don't get anything from my guy except a bill marked Paid." I switched over the following week and stuck with his replacement for a year. So the message here is simple—therapy can work if you have the patience to find the right fit and then stick with it.

Yoga, I've discovered, can be another weapon in the battle against clinical depression. Granted, you can't practice Downward Dog with sixty staples holding your surgical wound in place, but you might be able to later on. Meanwhile, you can practice the most important principles of yoga—breathing, meditation, patience, compassion, being present in the moment—anywhere at any time. I'd never had an interest in yoga before, as I was a treadmill and weight-circuit type until Lynn encouraged me to try it a few months after my second surgery. "It will help with everything you're missing—flexibility, balance, strength, and confidence," she explained. I couldn't imagine how, but at that point, I was willing to go on a little faith; plus, she was a six-year yoga veteran.

Today, nearly three years later, I practice four to five times a week, including two classes. It brings me a sense of calm and peace no matter what else is happening in my life. And yes, I can do a nice Downward Dog too.

Beyond therapy, yoga, and, if you're as fortunate as I was, an incredibly supportive partner, there is one more resource. It's powerful and effective and costs nothing, and you don't need training. Just a little change in attitude. Being a hospital patient, especially a cardiothoracic surgical type, means ultimate vulnerability. You're the object of whomever may walk into your room. Maybe it's lunch, maybe it's an unexpected procedure, maybe it's good news, maybe it's not-so-good news. In such a setting, one thing is pretty much certain—every deep-seated, repressed fear that's in you will come out, and the entire experience can be terrifying. It was for me, especially the first time around. So I tried to adjust my attitude in a few ways.

One, I rediscovered the power of giving. It's natural to be preoccupied with our own needs after surviving major surgery. We've been through *so* much, and typically, it takes a long time to regain the independence we used to have—or at least some degree of it. So we have to lean on others along the way, and that's okay. But while we're doing so, there's still room to show others the same kindness and compassion we ourselves need. For me, it meant connecting to a few of my roommates and a couple of nurses such as Diane to show them my gratitude and understanding.

I learned this during bereavement after Susie died when I joined an online support group. Others who reached out to me were an enormous help, but I found that my reaching out to them was just as meaningful and perhaps even more so. When I think about it, I realize that's because it allowed me to see myself as more than just a man with a loss, just as reaching out in the hospital reminded me that I was more than just a man with an illness.

Second, and this really took me a while, I got back in touch with my authentic self, the one who could make important decisions, such as returning to the hospital for my second surgery. I *chose* to do that and got the help I needed to make it happen. I could have avoided the whole thing, but instead, I *chose* to live.

The very ability to act autonomously allows us to feel more in control and therefore less helpless. It's easy to fall into depression when we feel powerless; conversely, it's uplifting to be proactive because we feel we matter. So I chose to drive again, do yoga, and travel even out of the country. To have a life. Maybe even a better life. No, not maybe. Definitely!

Printed and bound by PG in the USA